JAY HARRINGTON

—

THE

OutLaw

WRITER

HOW TO MAKE THE LEAP
from Practicing Lawyer
to Freelance Writer

ORDERING INFORMATION

For additional copies, visit www.hcommunications.biz/books or www.amazon.com. Quantity discounts available—for more information, visit www.outlawwriter.com or email the author at jay@hcommunications.biz.

ISBN

978-0-9995545-6-2

For more information, and free resources related to the book, visit **www.outlawwriter.com.**

TABLE OF CONTENTS

———

INTRODUCTION

W hat do you want? Who will you be? What will you be doing ten years from now? If you're a practicing lawyer who is dissatisfied in your current circumstances, will you make the changes necessary to pursue a more fulfilling path? Will you take the leap? Not a leap of faith, but rather a carefully considered transition to a new career that offers flexibility, growth potential, and the opportunity to put the skills you developed as a lawyer to productive use.

I remember the moment I began considering alternative careers quite clearly. I was sitting in my office late at night. I was a second-year associate at the Chicago office of an international law firm awaiting feedback from a partner on a brief that was due the next day. I had sent the draft out hours before. It gave me plenty of time to consider my future.

My discontent had nothing to do with the firm or my colleagues. It was a good job. I appreciated the benefits—high pay, prestige, challenging work, and robust support—that my position offered, and I genuinely liked the people I worked with. It was the 24/7, always-on daily grind of life at a big law firm that was tough to bear. I thought: *There has to be a better way to make a living.*

So I brainstormed. I grabbed a fresh legal pad and wrote at the top: Operation OutLaw. I jotted down business ideas. Like most ideas cooked up late at night, my bullet points led nowhere. The only business idea I remember jotting down involved starting a liquor store in Chicago that would feature nice design, live music, a large inventory of craft beer and bourbon, and cheese and wine tastings. As they say, follow your passions.

Four years later...I was still practicing law, albeit at a different law firm and in a new city. Not much had changed, including my ambivalence. I had a secure job. I was advancing. What was missing was enthusiasm and autonomy.

So I decided to take a leap. I pulled out another legal pad, but rather than trying to come up with a good business idea, I focused on what I liked to do—what I was passionate about—as a starting point. This exercise allowed me to spot a pattern: from my undergraduate study of journalism, to law school, to becoming a lawyer, it was clear that I was drawn to education and work settings that allowed me to write.

From a very young age, I was a voracious reader and loved writing short stories. Throughout my life, I unconsciously gravitated toward disciplines that involved writing. However, not once did I ever consider writing as a career option.

Perhaps my experience is similar to yours. Many people become lawyers because they are skilled at and enjoy writing. Without a clear understanding of what practicing law actually entails, they matriculate to law school because "philosopher" seems a bit impractical. Their only window into the world of law is through pop culture, so they envision a career writing thoughtful legal briefs and delivering rousing closing arguments to captivated jurors. Then they accept the job offer with the highest starting salary and reality sets in.

I viewed my second session with the legal pad as a chance to start over. And when it became clear to me that writing was my calling, I dug in to figure out how writers actually make a living.

I wasn't interested in finding another job. I wanted to be my own boss, set my own hours, and do work on my terms. Accordingly, a career in journalism or as a full-time writer for some big corporation wasn't an option. And there was no way I was going to become the next John Grisham, so writing books was out of the question. I had a mortgage to pay.

I came to discover that there was a cohort of writers, called freelance writers, who seemed to be thriving in what was increasingly becoming a "freelance economy" in the mid 2000s. Like lawyers, they were hired by businesses to work on projects for a fee, but all they had to do was write—not that writing for a living is easy and effortless, mind you, but more on that in the chapters to come. Some were technical writers. Others wrote marketing copy for ads and websites. Another group wrote thought-leadership content—articles, blog posts, and white papers—for professionals and executives.

At that time, there were far fewer freelance writers than there are today, mainly because there were far fewer opportunities. The commercial Internet was relatively new, and blogging was just becoming a thing, especially for businesses. The term "content marketing" was nowhere near as ubiquitous as it is today.

Across all disciplines and sectors of the economy, more people are engaging in freelance work. In 2020, according to data from Upwork, it is estimated that 57.3 million Americans (36 percent of the population) will earn income from freelance work, and by 2027, a majority of the U.S. workforce will consist of freelancers.[1]

As I was contemplating making the transition from a stable, well-paying job as a lawyer, to what seemed like a risky venture as a freelance writer, a single consideration spurred me on: I'd rather bet on myself, and live life on my terms, than rely upon the whims of an employer. After all, I concluded that having a diversified portfolio of clients would be more secure than counting on one employer.

Almost 15 years later, I can say with absolute confidence that it was the best business decision I ever made. I now have a business with a team of writers I work with. I live where I want. I work when I want. Admittedly, I don't earn as much money as I might have as a partner in a large law firm. But I'll accept that trade-off any day for the freedom of being my own boss and doing work I enjoy.

You may be perfectly content in your legal career, and if that's the case, that's great. The practice of law can be a deeply rewarding career. But let's face it, it's not for everyone.

Surveys suggest that career dissatisfaction among lawyers, and even rates of depression, are on the rise. According to 2018 research conducted by the Hazelden Betty Ford Foundation and the American Bar Association Commission on Lawyer Assistance Programs, 21 percent of licensed, employed attorneys qualify as problem drinkers, 28 percent struggle with depression, and 19 percent exhibit symptoms of anxiety. The greatest incidence of these problems occurs in younger lawyers in the first ten years of practice.[2]

If you're unhappy with your job, you're obviously not alone. And if you're looking for a new path, there are many options available to you. A legal education and experience practicing law provide great training for many different alternative careers. If you're exploring new opportunities, and enjoy stringing words together, I suggest you give serious consideration to pursuing writing as a vocation. In this book, I will explain the ins and outs of starting a freelance writing business, expound on why your background as a lawyer gives you a competitive advantage, and teach you how to market and sell your services effectively.

ONE

The Benefits of a Freelance Writing Career

———

L et's begin this journey by discussing some of the benefits and drawbacks of pursuing a career as a freelance writer. My life has significantly improved since I became a writer, as opposed to a practicing lawyer, and yours can, too. But I'm committed to being 100-percent transparent with you in this book, and there are definitely trade-offs—not all positive ones—that you will have to make in the process.

AUTONOMY

—

The worst part of law firm life for me was the lack of autonomy. My schedule felt out of my control. The demands of the job were often overwhelming. Clients expected 24/7 responsiveness. An unwelcome email, phone call, or pleading from an adversary on a Friday afternoon could turn a weekend upside down.

I believe that lack of autonomy is at the root of most discontent in the legal profession. It's no surprise that so many lawyers are unhappy with their circumstances, because research shows that "autonomy"—the feeling that your life, activities, and habits are self-chosen and self-endorsed—is the number one predictor of happiness for people.[3]

Freelance writers have tremendous autonomy. Sure, writers still have clients to deal with, but the stakes aren't as high and there are far fewer fire drills. You can generally make your own schedule, and take on as much or as little work as you want at any given time. Since it's just you and your laptop, you can scale your business up or down depending on your circumstances.

I know a number of attorneys who left the practice of law to start writing careers around the time they started families because the commitment required by their jobs prevented them from spending time with their kids. By freelancing, they stayed connected to the part of their former job they enjoyed—the writing—while maintaining a more flexible schedule.

In my experience, the ability to customize my schedule has helped immensely in getting through life's rough patches. From going from one child to three after the birth of our twin daughters, to settling in after a major move, being in control of my circumstances has been a real blessing. And it feels great to take a one-week vacation without worrying about an issue blowing up at the office. As your own boss, you make the rules.

However, being your own boss has its drawbacks. As a lawyer, your primary job is to bill hours and do quality work for clients. Your firm takes care of almost everything else, from bringing in work to replacing printer cartridges. Those tasks, and a hundred more like them, will rest on your shoulders as a business owner. As much as you aspire to be a writer, in order to write you must be willing to embrace the mundane and monotonous tasks that come along with running a business. That means tracking your expenses for tax filings, prospecting for clients, and dealing with vendors, among other things. If you're diligent and organized, handling the administrative aspects of a freelancing writing business won't take much time, and you'll spend the great majority of your time writing, but it's important to know that more than *just* writing is required.

WORK (AND LIVE) WHERE YOU WANT

One of the best aspects of freelance writing is that you can work where you want, live where you want, and structure your days how you want. No more daily commutes. No more drab offices. No more boring meetings. You can build your work around your life, and not your life around your work.

As a lawyer, your decision to live in a particular location may have been driven, to a large extent, by its proximity to your office. As a freelance writer, your office is wherever you happen to be at the moment. Face-to-face meetings with clients are rarely required. Zoom works just fine. As the economy continues to become more digital, more cloud-based, and more comfortable with remote-working arrangements, writers will continue to become more location independent.

I've lived in big cities and suburbs, but after starting a family my wife and I realized that we wanted to experience a different lifestyle. We desired a slower pace, more open space, and a closer connection to the great outdoors. In 2015, we moved to our "happy place," a small town on the shores of Lake Michigan in northwest Michigan called Traverse City. It's where we spent as much time as we could on vacation, and hoped to retire there some day.

After becoming location independent, we decided it made no sense to wait for retirement to live where we ultimately wanted to be, so we packed up and moved. Only after moving to our desired location did we come to realize the power of *place*—the impact that where you live has on well-being. We've never been happier.

I continue to serve a nationwide roster of writing, coaching and consulting clients from our small town. Clients never ask where I live. They don't care where my work is being done, as long as it's being done at a high level of quality. Best of all, since I mostly serve clients located in big cities, I can charge "big-city fees" while enjoying small-town cost of living. I know I deliver work product that is on par with the best in my industry, so why should my fees have any relation to geography? They shouldn't, and neither should yours.

As a freelance writer, you can take advantage of "geoarbitrage," a concept popularized by Tim Ferriss in his book *The 4-Hour Workweek*. By living in an area with low cost of living, and serving clients across the country who are accustomed to paying rates that are common in their metropolitan locales, you can make your dollars go further and enhance your lifestyle in the process.

Even if you have no desire or ability to move, freelancing still offers lifestyle advantages. You can work from home or at your local coffee shop. You can change things up throughout the day to keep things fresh. You can also take extended vacations, domestically or internationally, and mix in work with travel.

Of course, being location independent, and working for yourself and by yourself, is not for everyone. Freelancing can be lonely. You won't be surrounded by colleagues in a traditional workplace, and you will need to be proactive about connecting with others to avoid feeling isolated. You will also have to be more rigorous and disciplined about establishing a routine for yourself to ensure the distractions of home don't hinder your work.

Fortunately, evaluating whether an untethered work arrangement is right for you is likely easier than it would have been a few years ago, as almost every lawyer has experienced what it's like to work away from the office during the COVID-19 pandemic. You now have real-world experience to draw upon when considering your preferences.

In short, having the ability to work from anywhere can cut both ways. In my experience, the autonomy it fosters outweighs the possibility of feeling isolated. I miss the camaraderie of working closely with colleagues in an office. But I still have a strong community of colleagues that I interact with daily—and it's one of my own choosing.

PURSUE YOUR PASSION FOR WRITING

Approaching the age of 30, John Grisham was busy with his legal career, working 60 to 70 hours a week at a law firm in a small town in Mississippi. He specialized in criminal defense and personal injury litigation.[4]

At court one day, Grisham overheard the chilling testimony of a 12-year-old girl who had been raped. As a new dad, Grisham became fixated on the story and began to wonder what would have happened if the girl's father had taken matters into his own hands and killed her rapists. He decided to write a novel inspired by the story he heard in the DeSoto County courthouse that day.

Grisham could not afford to stop practicing law to pursue what he perceived as a writing hobby. He had a vision to become a successful author. His goal was to write and publish his first book. What he needed was a plan to make it happen in the midst of his hectic life.

To achieve his goal, Grisham created a daily ritual for himself. He would wake up at 5 a.m. sharp, take a quick shower, and hustle to his office. He would be at his desk, coffee and legal pad in hand, by 5:30 a.m. As with most busy litigators, Grisham would often have to be in court or in client meetings by no later than 9 a.m., so he knew those early hours would be critical for making progress.

His goal was to write at least one page per day. Three years later, by sticking to his rigorous daily writing routine, Grisham finished writing and editing his first novel, *A Time to Kill*. While his first book was a bit of a dud when it launched, he kept writing and ultimately achieved massive success—and left the practice of law behind—after his second book, *The Firm*, was published. He has since gone on to sell over 300 million books.

Because lawyers tend to be smart, curious, and possess strong writing skills, it comes as no surprise that many desire to write a book. In fact, polls suggest that approximately 80 percent of all people want to write a book, but few ever do.[5]

Grisham, Scott Turow, and others have managed to walk the tightrope and publish acclaimed books while practicing law, but they are outliers. Writing a book is taxing and requires consistent effort, so it's not something that fits neatly into a lawyer's busy schedule.

If you're contemplating a transition to a freelance writing career, you may be motivated by the idea of doing more writing for yourself, such as working on a book or starting a blog, while also writing for clients. A flexible freelance schedule can allow you to explore such creative pursuits. By doing more writing work for clients, you will produce better writing results for yourself. Plus, writing for clients at the same time you're working on a passion project will relieve financial pressures, which will help unlock your creativity. Most writers have to strike some sort of balance between writing for themselves and writing for clients. Finding the right balance will make you better. Writing is like physical exercise. The more consistently and rigorously you do it, the stronger you will become at it.

Unless it was a memo or a brief, I rarely wrote when I was a practicing lawyer. I simply didn't have the mental or physical capacity—and, therefore, the motivation—to do any creative work outside of my job. Since leaving to become a full-time writer, in addition to my writing work for clients, I've written four business nonfiction books and one children's book, created two blogs, and produced hundreds of articles for several publications, including Law. com, Attorney at Work, and JD Supra. Once I got into the routine of writing, the volume of work I was able to produce increased dramatically.

If you have an idea for a creative writing project, be it a book or a blog, the best way to make it happen is to get into a writing habit that creates a virtuous cycle. The writing work you do for clients as a freelancer will make your creative writing better, and vice versa. The more you write, the more you will write.

The only potential downside I see to pursuing personal writing projects is when someone has unrealistic expectations going into the process. It's noisy out there. People have almost infinite options when deciding what content to consume, and much of it is available for free. Writers, like all content creators, must cultivate an audience over time. There are examples of writers bursting onto the scene with a blockbuster first novel. But that's the exception, not the rule.

The unfortunate truth is that most writers have to give away lots of content (they create blogs, they write articles for other publications) before they are in a position to charge for their work. That's why I recommend that aspiring writers do paid writing work for clients—freelance writing—while pursuing writing projects they're passionate about. The notion of the "starving artist" has been romanticized, but any writer will tell you that they're incapable of doing their best work if they don't know how they're going to put food on the table.

CHAPTER 1

TWO

Walking Away from the Legal Profession

———

I know that some significant percentage, perhaps a strong majority, of those who read this book will not leave the practice of law to pursue a writing career. I'm okay with that—and if you make the decision to continue in your legal career, you should be too. My job is to present perspective, options and information. It's not to push anyone in a particular direction.

My objective is certainly not to convince you that becoming a lawyer was a bad decision, that the practice of law is a dead end, or that the grass is always greener on the other side. In fact, I believe that the practice of law is a great and noble profession. Lawyers are in a unique position to make a positive difference in other people's lives. They have an opportunity to earn a good living to support themselves and their families. I worked with many happy, well-adjusted and successful lawyers when I practiced law. Now, as a coach and consultant I deal with many other lawyers who are wholly content.

I would never second guess someone's decision to continue practicing law. In writing this book, I've set out to propose an alternative for those who have concluded that they no longer want to be a lawyer—or their life circumstances don't allow them to be a lawyer—but don't know what path to follow next. After reading this book, you may decide that your next best move is not to make a move at all, and there are many good reasons why you might reach that conclusion, including:

- You have financial obligations, such as law school loans, that you want to pay off before pursuing a new career. For many people, that's a wise decision, because there is a strong likelihood that most lawyers who shift to freelance writing will have to take a pay cut—at least temporarily.

- You're intrigued by the idea of becoming a full-time writer, but have other interests you want to explore before taking the leap. As a lawyer, you have a skill set that many employers in other fields find attractive, and you may have an idea for another business, so it doesn't hurt to keep your options open.

- You may decide that you can continue practicing law and still scratch the writing itch. Some lawyers, like

best-selling author Scott Turow of Jenner & Block,
are able to maintain successful legal practices while
writing well-regarded books.

In my business coaching practice, I have worked with many lawyers in the throes of trying to figure out whether to switch careers. Some want to start businesses, while others want to teach or write. I don't push them in one direction or the other. As their coach, my job is to ask tough questions, challenge assumptions, and help my clients see issues from every angle. I don't tell them what to do, despite the fact that many would prefer to outsource the difficult decision of whether to stay or to go.

While the role of a coach is to help others find the answers within themselves—to "trip over the truth"—I fervently push back on one common argument for staying: maintaining the status quo merely because it feels like so much time and effort has already been invested in one's education and career. As I stated, there are many good reasons to decide not to leave the practice of law. But staying put merely because of past expenditures of time and resources is a fallacious justification that almost always leads to regret.

HAVE THE COURAGE TO MOVE BEYOND SUNK COSTS

The "sunk cost fallacy" is a common cause of poor decision-making, and decisions about work and careers are no exception. A "sunk cost" is any past cost of money, time or effort that cannot be recovered. The investment has been made and there is no getting it back. This fallacy arises in many different ways. Ever start a book, get bored halfway through, but plow on to the end nonetheless? The two hours you spent reading shouldn't influence your decision about investing even more time in something that's not worthwhile, but it often does. The more energy or resources we devote to something, the harder it is to abandon it.

If it's difficult to put down a bad book, you can see why sunk costs influence many lawyers' decisions to stick with the practice of law despite wanting, deep down, to pursue something else.

It's hard to walk away from something you've worked so hard for. When you're contemplating an important decision, such as whether to leave the practice of law, you'll almost certainly question yourself about the wisdom of walking away from the pay and social prestige associated with your job. A big part of your angst will not just be negative self-talk, but also the expectations and feedback of others. Other people—family, friends and random strangers—will tell you that you're crazy for contemplating (as they likely see it) throwing your law school diploma in the trash to become a writer.

A season-three episode of the hit show *Better Call Saul* captures the type of conversations you're likely to have with those in your inner circle once you let them in on your desire for change. In the episode, Saul, who is a struggling lawyer trying to make ends meet, decides to ditch the practice of law right after receiving a job offer at a prestigious law firm. Over drinks, his friend Kim confronts him with the obvious: How can you walk away now? "All that effort, you're just going to toss it away?" Kim says.

"That's a sunk cost fallacy," Saul responds. "It's what gamblers do. They throw good money after bad, thinking they can turn their luck around." He explains that his talents "are better suited elsewhere."

Don't jump blindly out of the law and into something new. But also don't continue throwing more good money after bad. Once you understand the sunk cost fallacy and its implications, you can think more clearly about the decision you face, focused on the future not the past, and free from self doubt sown by those questioning your judgment.

WHATEVER YOU DO, DON'T LOOK BACK WITH REGRET

Take your time in contemplating the decision that lies before you. Weigh the pros and cons, and consider the thoughtful input you receive, but at the end of the day, you will have to make a gut decision. There's no way to know what an alternative future holds for you, although you have a pretty good sense of what the status quo will lead to. The worst outcome is that you look back, years from now, with regret for what could have been for the one life you've been given.

Bronnie Ware is a palliative nurse in Australia. She spent years counseling and caring for patients on their deathbeds. During the course of her work, she began to record the regrets of those at the end of their lives, and chronicled them in a book called *The Top Five Regrets of the Dying*. The most common regret was this:

"I wish I'd had the courage to live a life true to myself, not the life others expected of me."

Everyone should periodically reexamine their choices and direction because life goes fast, and we all have a tendency to settle into comfortable routines. Despite the comfort and familiarity of the status quo, there may be a road less traveled worth exploring that leads to a destination more aligned with your long-term objectives. Even if an alternate path seems scary and fraught with risk, the risk of the status quo may be even greater. Research shows that more people regret the things they didn't do than those they did, even if things didn't turn out the way they expected.[6]

The odds are the longer you continue to practice law, the less likely it will be that you leave to try something new. The further along the partnership track you get, the more invested you will be to keep going. The more you become accustomed to living and spending like a lawyer, the more the "golden handcuffs" will tighten their grip on you. The longer you associate your identity as that of a lawyer, the harder it will be to shed that identity and cloak yourself in a new one.

You may continue to hold out hope, whether consciously or unconsciously, that some externality will force you to make a decision; that something will occur that will compel you to act. And that may happen, as it did for Susan Cain, who left the practice of law to write *The New York Times* monster bestseller *Quiet: The Power of Introverts in a World That Can't Stop Talking*.

Cain discussed her transition out of the practice of law and into a writing career on Tim Ferriss's podcast. She graduated from Harvard Law School and spent almost seven years as an associate at a Wall Street law firm. Cain described herself as an "ambivalent corporate lawyer, at best." Nonetheless, she dedicated herself to her career. One afternoon, the senior partner in her firm informed her that she wouldn't be put up for partner on schedule. Upon hearing the news, Cain burst into tears in front of him.

Crestfallen, she immediately asked for a leave of absence. She spent the rest of the day bicycling around New York City, with no idea of what to do next. Then a critical realization occurred to her that changed the course of her life: She remembered she had always wanted to be a writer. She began writing that evening. She explained to Ferriss on his podcast: "From then on, writing would be my center, and I would look for freelance work that would allow me lots of free time to pursue it."[7]

Cain used an apparent failure as the triggering event to propel her into her new career as a writer. "If I had succeeded at making partner, right on schedule, I might still be miserably negotiating corporate transactions 16 hours a day. It's not that I had never thought about what else I might like to do other than law, but until I had space and time to think about life outside of the hermetic culture of a law practice, I couldn't figure out what I really wanted to do," Cain said.

Like Cain, you can wait for some intervening force to compel you to determine what you really want to do. However, the day when a partner or personal circumstance leaves you no choice but to examine your path may never come. Or if it does, it might be too late to do anything about it. Be proactive. Take control of the process yourself. It's easy to get caught up in the whirlwind of the day-to-day practice of law. Don't drift aimlessly. Again, after thoughtful introspection, you may determine that you're on the right track. But you'll never know until you really consider what you want in the future and explore alternatives to the status quo.

If you decide to leave the practice of law, don't lament the time you spent in law school and at the office as time wasted. Treat it for what it was: an invaluable investment in your future.

Susan Cain doesn't regret the seven years she practiced law. In fact, she thinks her experience as a lawyer has been integral to her success as a lawyer, providing her with a window into the "real world" of business and helping her to build a financial cushion that removed some of the pressure from her creative pursuits. Similarly, if you leave the law, your education and experience as a lawyer will not go to waste. You will be in the unique position to apply all of the skills and knowledge you learned as a lawyer to a new domain.

While navigating what lies ahead will not be easy nor free of uncertainty, one thing is clear: Your decisions should not be based on how much you have invested in the past, but rather what you stand to gain in the future.

"NOBODY KNOWS ANYTHING"

———

When I left the practice of law to become a writer, it was a clean break. On a Friday afternoon, I left my well-appointed law firm office for the last time, and on the following Monday morning I sat down in my new office, a small room in shared office space, to start my new "job." I fiddled for a bit, shuffling paper on my desk and cleaning up my computer desktop. It wasn't long before the fear and self-doubt hit me. I thought: *What the hell did I just do?* I left a good job—a job that I was good at—to become a writer.

A *writer*? What does that even mean?

I had a few writing projects lined up, but not nearly enough to pay the bills. Like Susan Cain, I had a small financial cushion to fall back on, but it wouldn't last for long. Had I put my family at risk? Would I soon be pleading to get my old job back? I'm not a writer, I thought to myself, I'm a lawyer. *What had I done?*

I spent some time spiraling, but finally got a grip. Everything worked out in the end, as things tend to do. What helped me get over the hump was the realization that

I had felt that way—scared, uncertain, and doubting my abilities—many times before. I remembered the terror I felt walking onto the baseball field as a scrawny 18-year-old freshman, joining my teammates—many of whom were 22-year-old grown men—for the first practice of my college baseball career. I recalled the angst I experienced as a first-year lawyer at a big, busy law firm. I was constantly in over my head.

But in those instances and others, I ultimately figured things out. It all ended up okay. The lessons I learned while navigating challenges in the past gave me confidence that I could overcome new challenges associated with becoming a writer, too.

Should you leave the practice of law to become a writer, you will likely experience similar doubts about your decision. It's not an easy transition. You will need to get past the feeling that you don't belong in your new profession, and ignore the voice in your head that tells you you're not good enough.

While that voice cuts you down, it also builds others up. It tells you that those around you are smarter, better and more talented than you are and that they have it all figured out. If you listen to the voice, you end up staying safely within your comfort zone and stop taking risks. Your forward momentum stalls. Your confidence wanes. You start to question your judgment. When the voice gets really loud, it engenders fear that is paralyzing. For some, it's powerful enough to stop them from pursuing their passions, such as becoming a writer, altogether.

Psychologists Pauline Clance and Suzanne Imes call this type of fear "imposter syndrome." They describe it as a feeling of "phoniness in people who [fear they] are not intelligent, capable or creative despite evidence of high achievement." They "live in fear of being 'found out' or exposed as frauds."

You may—likely will—feel like an imposter at some point as you transition into a new career as a writer. An important step in overcoming this hurdle is realizing that we are all imposters. No one knows what he or she is doing most of the time. As screenwriter William Goldman said, "Nobody knows anything."

For people who routinely step out of their comfort zones, uncertainty is a constant. This is true for lawyers, writers and titans of industry. In an interview with *The New York Times*, Starbucks founder Howard Schultz said, "Very few people, whether you've been in that job before or not, get into the seat and believe today that they are now qualified to be the CEO. They're not going to tell you that, but it's true."

We are always changing and evolving. We have the capacity to learn and apply new skills. Every time we take on a new challenge, we are forced to adapt. If we feel comfortable, it means we are not learning and growing. In this sense, feeling like an imposter is a positive signal. It's something to lean into, not shrink away from.

While it may not be possible to rid oneself of imposter-like feelings, there are ways to lessen their negative implications. To tackle a difficult challenge, such as building a successful freelance writing business, you must change your identity—your belief about who you are and want to become. Before you can do the difficult work necessary to become someone new, you must form the fundamental belief that the change you seek is possible.

As you begin your transformation from a lawyer to a writer, it's critical that you begin to see yourself as a writer. Your actions will then follow your beliefs. Every time you take action in accordance with your beliefs, you embody the identity you seek. When you fail to take action, you reinforce the belief that you're not capable or worthy of the outcome. Even if you're just getting started, you must act "as if" you are what you want to become.

If you want to be a writer, you must write. Write in a journal. Start a blog. It's as simple as that. If you're not ready to share your writing with the world, write only for yourself. Stop thinking about what you want, and start doing it, even if it only feels like a tiny step forward. Transformation is a two-step process. First, define who you want to become. Second, reinforce your identity through consistent small actions.

John Grisham believed he could become a writer. He reinforced that belief by acting as if he was a writer—he wrote at least one page every day. That's what writers do. As a result, he finished his first book. More importantly, through his belief in himself and his commitment to write every day, he established a writing habit that allowed him to go on to become a prolific international best-selling author. Amateur writers wait for inspiration. Professionals take action.

Across domains, when people fail to achieve their goals, it's typically because their desire for an end result is not matched by a commitment to do what it takes to get there. Everyone wants the result—the gold medal, the rewarding relationship, the best-selling book, the profitable client—but few are willing to put in the hard work that precedes the result. Those who fall short harbor a limiting belief that they're not capable or deserving of the outcomes they seek.

As you set out on your writing journey, start small and trust that results will come as you form a new identity. Get yourself prepared. Learn what it takes to succeed. Lay the groundwork. Write every day, even if for an audience of one. The only way to become a professional writer is to start acting as if you are one. Your actions will follow your identity.

OVERCOME THE MENTAL HURDLES

Change is hard. You will doubt yourself every step of the way as you transition to a freelance writing career. Family and friends will question your judgment. If you're not mentally strong, you won't make it.

Don't aim for massive change all at once. The more you rush, the more likely you are to revert to your equilibrium—the life of a practicing lawyer. Your goal should be sustainable change. Progress comes when you take slow, steady steps forward. The fact that you're reading this book suggests you're serious about tackling what lies ahead. Here are some other ways to gain insight, confidence and experience.

Start Writing. I don't know about you, but I rarely know what to think about something until I write about it. Writing is what allows us to process information, synthesize our thoughts, and become more persuasive.

Many successful people write every day, and not always for public consumption. Writing in a journal or on a blog forces you to clarify and articulate your thoughts. It's not easy to start a daily writing practice, but it becomes easier over time.

In short, the most tangible and effective way to gain an understanding of whether the writer's life is for you is to establish a daily writing routine. Write something every day, other than legal briefs. Spend five minutes in the morning writing in a journal in order to work through the mental hurdles you're facing, or to plan out the next steps in your career transition. Tackle a thought-leadership article at work. Create a Medium account and start writing posts about something you're passionate about. Keep it simple. Don't put too much pressure on yourself. Simply get into the practice of writing.

Read Books. Want to learn more about writing and what it takes to succeed as a writer? Read Stephen King's *On Writing*, Steven Pressfield's *The War of Art*, and Anne Lamott's *Bird by Bird*. These books are a pleasure to read and are packed with insights for aspiring writers.

Read other great books, too. Charlie Munger, legendary lawyer and vice chairman of Berkshire Hathaway, advises: "Develop into a lifelong self-learner through voracious reading; cultivate curiosity and strive to become a little wiser every day."

There is a symbiotic relationship between reading and writing. The more you read, the more you'll recognize great writing. The more you write, the more you'll want to read, because you'll learn through osmosis how to improve your writing.

According to Stephen King, "If you want to be a writer, you must do two things above all others: read a lot and write a lot. There's no way around those two things that I'm aware of, no shortcut."

Find Your "Scene." In the 1920s, Ernest Hemingway moved to Paris to join a scene of expatriate writers and artists, including F. Scott Fitzgerald, who had taken up residence in the Left Bank. Members of this "Lost Generation" hung out at cafés, argued about politics, caroused late into the night on the streets of Paris, and produced some of the greatest works of literature of the 20th century. They leaned on each other to push and prod themselves through challenges and to higher levels of performance. They were better together than they would have been trying to work in isolation. You can similarly benefit from finding and associating with others who stand in your shoes and are seeking answers to the same questions you are facing. That's easier said than done, however, when you're immersed in a busy law firm environment.

You must look outside the walls of your law firm to find a scene. Connect with other freelance writers on LinkedIn. Join a local writing group. Seek out a writing mentor. As motivational speaker Jim Rohn famously said: "We are the average of the five people we spend the most time with." Spend more time with other writers.

Looking to make connections with other writers? An easy way to start is by joining the OutLaw Writer Academy, which consists of aspiring lawyers-turned-writers like you. You'll be part of a small cohort of people who receive training, get their questions answered, share resources, and private support to one another. To join, visit: www.outlawwriter.com.

DON'T LEAP WITHOUT A NET

If you're not happy practicing law, and looking to make a change, you're probably anxious to dive into something new. Don't rush into your next move with abandon. It's important to have a safety net in place for yourself. The surest way to start doubting your decision to become a writer is if you're feeling stressed about your finances.

If you're a practicing lawyer who is earning a salary, it will take time and hard work to replace your income through freelance writing. It's possible to earn as much or more as a writer as you do as a lawyer, but it will not happen overnight. It may take years of effort. If you have a financial nest egg or income-earning partner you can rely on then you may be in a position to dive right in. Otherwise, to make it easier on yourself, consider various ways you can relieve the financial burden.

One option is to start writing as a side hustle. At a minimum, start writing for yourself so you can exercise your writing muscle and build a portfolio of work. Ideally, try to generate a few clients and work on projects at night or on the weekends.

Another alternative that will allow you to pursue more freelance writing is to also pursue freelance legal work. Advances in technology, changing preferences about the nature of a legal career, and shifts in perceptions about how to maximize the value of legal spending have converged to create more mobile, on-demand legal "gigs" that are creating new opportunities up and down the legal ecosystem. A growing number of alternative legal service providers provide flexibility-seeking lawyers with options to do freelance legal work for law firms and corporate legal departments remotely and on a short-term basis. Such opportunities can help you build the financial bridge you need to get to a full-time freelance writing career.

You can realize your dream of becoming a writer, but it won't happen overnight. You need to be smart and strategic about your approach, especially as it relates to your financial circumstances. Finding ways to supplement your income, even if it means keeping one foot in the practice of law, will make the transition much easier.

THREE

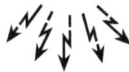

Enter Into a Contract
with Yourself

—

magine you are representing a client in a business dispute. Your client is a small parts manufacturer that is struggling in its relationship with one of its largest customers. The parts your client supplies to its customer are critical. They can't easily be procured from another supplier. Nonetheless, the customer is slow to pay, frequently seeks discounts, and routinely and unjustifiably rejects shipments of parts on the basis that they are not up to spec.

Your client can't simply walk away from the relationship

because the customer accounts for a significant percentage of its revenue. But it also can't sustain the status quo because the customer's actions are eating away at your client's profitability and all the problems are consuming a tremendous amount of time and resources.

You have been brought in to broker a solution. You prepare a letter outlining your client's concerns, and detail your client's rights and its customer's obligations under the relevant purchase and supply agreement. You propose a meeting to hash out the issues.

A meeting takes place with you, your client, the customer and its legal counsel in attendance. It goes well, at least from your client's perspective. The customer provides assurances about performance and floats the idea that it may increase its orders in the future. The meeting concludes and your client shakes hands with the customer representative. As far as your client is concerned, the matter is resolved.

You, of course, know that there is an important next step, which is documenting the parties' discussion in a written and signed agreement. Your client is wary. He suggests that he is comfortable with his customer's representations, and "doesn't want to ruffle any feathers." You push back hard, but he is insistent.

For a few weeks, the customer lives up to its promises. It doesn't take long, however, for the situation to regress. Because your client relied on assurances and a handshake, he is left with little recourse.

As lawyers, we know that we should always "get it in writing" on behalf of our clients. But when it comes to ourselves? Just like our clients, we tend to be too trusting of loose promises—especially when we make promises to ourselves.

I'm going to lose weight, learn to play an instrument, or

pursue that new career opportunity.

We tell ourselves that we are finally going to take action, but fail to follow through. Every time we fail, we reinforce the idea that we are incapable of transformational change.

Lack of desire and motivation is not the problem. We want the outcome. We just don't know how to achieve it. Typically, the enormity of the task we face simply overwhelms us, so we never get started. The way around this problem is to think small. The bigger the task the more important it is to take it step by step...or bird by bird.

At the end of Chapter 2, I recommended that you read Anne Lamott's book *Bird by Bird*. It's an honest, insightful and funny book on writing. The title comes from Lamott's childhood and serves as a metaphor for how to take on a big challenge—from writing a book to starting a writing career. Here is the key passage:

> *"Thirty years ago my older brother, who was ten years old at the time, was trying to get a report on birds written that he'd had three months to write, which was due the next day. We were out at our family cabin in Bolinas, and he was at the kitchen table, close to tears, surrounded by binder paper and pencils and unopened books on birds, immobilized by the hugeness of the task ahead. Then my father sat down beside him, put his arm around my brother's shoulder, and said, 'Bird by bird, buddy. Just take it bird by bird.'"*

You may be intimidated and overwhelmed by the idea of leaving the law to pursue writing. I sure was. The way that I, and others, overcame what felt like a massive, insurmountable challenge was to break it down into a series of small steps. To reach the destination you seek you need to formulate a plan. You need to conquer your fears and take steps forward, "bird by bird."

And, importantly, you need to get it in writing. If you're serious about this journey, if you're committed to this change, you need to enter into a contract with yourself that holds you accountable to the promises you make to yourself. Without such a contract, it will be easy to let yourself off the hook. Granted, when you make a contract with yourself, you're the jury of one who is left to render judgment as to whether you lived up to your obligations, but the mere act of writing down your objectives significantly increases your odds of achieving them. Self-accountability happens the moment you commit on paper your intent to reach an objective. Research shows that reducing your goals—your contract with yourself—to writing significantly increases your chances of achieving your objectives.

Gail Matthews, a psychology professor at Dominican University in California, did a study on goal-setting with 267 participants from a wide range of professions and countries. She found that people are over 40 percent more likely to achieve their goals when they write them down.[8] In his best-selling book, *The Power of Habit: Why We Do What We Do in Life and Business*, Charles Duhigg discusses a study in which patients recovering from knee or hip surgery were given a booklet and instructed to write down their recovery goals and a detailed action plan to achieve them. Three months later, the patients who wrote down their goals were walking well before those who did not. They recovered almost twice as fast.

One of key reasons it's important to create a written plan of action—which I will explain in detail shortly—is to help you make the transition from merely learning about becoming a freelance writer to taking action.

Knowledge may be power, but not if it comes at the expense of action. Just as too much stuff in your garage prevents you from pulling your car in, too much stuff in your head can prevent you from moving forward in pursuit of your most important goals in life.

When starting a business or pursuing a new vocation, there's a foundational amount of knowledge you need to acquire before moving forward.

Let's say you're in the early stages of the process, so you start doing research online. There are millions of articles that address the many facets of entrepreneurship. You read, and read, and read, hurtling down rabbit hole after rabbit hole. Some advice inspires you. Then something else contradicts it. Next thing you know, six months have passed and you're right where you started. Frustrated by your lack of progress, and twisted into knots by everything you've read and learned, you give up, vowing to start anew in six months. And by that time, you're more deeply rooted in the status quo, and there is a mountain of new information to digest. It's paralyzing.

Learning, in and of itself, is not particularly helpful, except as an intellectual exercise or for purposes of cocktail hour fodder. Selective learning, followed by relentless implementation of what you've learned, is the path to progress.

The pursuit of knowledge can be a crutch as well. It feels like action, but it's not. For instance, it feels good to be inspired while learning about a great new kettlebell routine, but it's not going to get you the toned body you desire. That only comes (so I've heard) from cranking out reps at the gym.

Trial and error in the real world is the best method of learning. But learning is not "trial." And while you'll avoid "error" if all you ever do is learn, you'll never get where you want to go. There is only one way forward, and it is through action—imperfect as it might be.

FROM VISION TO ACTION

John Grisham didn't simply wake up one day, decide he wanted to be a writer, quit his job, and start pecking away at the keyboard. He made a plan for himself that allowed him to financially sustain himself, and found time to work on his books early in the morning before starting his legal work. Susan Cain quit her job to become a writer, but she only did so after amassing a financial cushion, and she built up a freelance business that provided her income while she spent seven years writing her first book.

While the experiences of Grisham and Cain are not completely on point (although you may desire to write a book and freelance writing is a great way to subsidize your efforts) it is nonetheless instructive. In particular, both Grisham and Cain crafted a clear vision of what they wanted in the future and then started taking action. To become a freelance writer, you must do the same.

Vision. When tackling any difficult, long-term challenge, success starts with getting clear on what you want—way out in the future—so you can know what steps are required, starting today, to move forward. Do you want to become a partner at a law firm in five years? If so, then it makes sense to keep working those 50-hour weeks. If not? Well, then it's time to get clear on your long-term vision so you stop wasting time and start taking action that is aligned with your vision.

Your vision is the mental picture of the result you want to achieve. It is critical to craft a clear vision for the future

CHAPTER 3

because it is what inspires action today. A vision is not a vague wish or dream—it is a concrete mental model of what is possible in the future. A vision also serves as a guide for taking action.

The first step in creating a contract with yourself is casting a clear vision. Your vision for the future is the preamble to the contract. If you have a clear vision of where you want to go in the future, you will not be distracted and derailed in your journey. Consider the following prompts to help you craft your personal Vision Statement:

- Describe your ideal life and career in five years.

- What will you have achieved?

- What metric(s) will you be using to measure success?

- How will life and work be different?

The objective of this exercise is to envision and describe not only what you will have accomplished, but also who you will have become, over the next five years. Aim to complete this exercise in no more than four to five sentences.

Casting a vision for your future requires clear thinking and an investment of time. You need to be able to envision and articulate your ideal future before you can start working toward it. Create a Vision Statement. Begin by defining what your ideal life and career looks like five years down the road, then describe what you stand to gain—what it will feel like, what you will have achieved—when you realize your vision.

Goals. The words vision and goal are not synonymous. A vision (for example, becoming a successful freelance writer who earns a good income and sets her own schedule) is the destination you want to reach. The destination may be clear, but the path to get there is not. Goals allow you to determine the path you must travel to realize your vision, and they serve as milestones along the way. A vision is the end. Goals are the means.

To reinforce the distinction between vision and goals, and highlight its importance, let's examine the approach of the man who is arguably the most successful entrepreneur of our time, if not all time: Jeff Bezos, CEO of Amazon and founder of aerospace company Blue Origin.

Bezos has cast bold visions for both companies. In 1995, while operating Amazon out of his garage, Bezos crafted an ambitious vision statement for Amazon in which he stated his intention to grow it into the "Earth's most customer-centric company."

In a speech at the Yale Club in New York City in 2019, Bezos explained that his mission for Blue Origin is to help create a way for the solar system to support 1 trillion people. That way, Bezos said, "we'd have 1,000 Mozarts, and 1,000 Einsteins."

Now that's some bold thinking. However, while Bezos recognized in his speech that "vision is absolutely important," he explained that it wasn't enough. To realize his vision for his companies, Bezos said, "we've got to get started." Getting started requires setting clear goals that, once achieved, will move you closer to realizing your vision.

In the case of Amazon, its efforts to offer a huge inventory of products at the lowest prices possible, one- or two-day delivery of products, the Kindle, its foray into groceries through its acquisition of Whole Foods, and a broad array of other initiatives, all resulted from goals Amazon set with its vision of becoming the "Earth's most customer-centric company" in mind.

"You need a vision, then, that's a touchstone. It's something you can always come back to if you ever get confused," Bezos said. "But mostly, your time should be spent on things that are happening today, this year, maybe in the next two to three years."

As Bezos has demonstrated through his visionary leadership, setting a goal that is ambitious, specific, and measurable allows you to both confirm your intentions and begin taking steps toward transformational change. Goal-setting is one of the most powerful tools you have at your disposal, no matter what you want to achieve in life. Virtually all coaches, corporate trainers, business leaders and other experts use goal-setting as a key component of their processes to push others toward higher performance. And you should set goals in order to push yourself.

Don't worry if you've had trouble making progress on your goals in the past. That's an experience everyone can relate to. Consider this an opportunity to start anew.

With your Vision Statement in mind (if you haven't yet written down your Vision Statement, I encourage you to do so now), it's time to start thinking about reducing that vision into actionable goals. Goals help put the realization of your vision on a deadline.

The most well-known and, in my experience, effective technique for setting and achieving goals is the SMART-goal framework, which is often attributed to the work of management consultant Peter Drucker. "SMART" stands for Specific, Measurable, Attainable, Realistic, and Time-bound.

One of the key benefits of using the SMART-goal framework is that it forces you to clearly consider and define goals as you set them, thereby reducing the risk of creating vague, ambiguous goals that are unlikely to be achieved.

A SMART goal must be:

Specific: The more detailed and specific your goals are, the more likely you'll be to achieve them. Think about the last time you hired a vendor to complete a job in your home or delegated an assignment to someone in your workplace. If your instructions were vague, did you get the results you were hoping for? Probably not, and the same principle applies to goal-setting. With SMART goals, you're providing instructions to yourself, so be specific. How specific should your goal be? "I will become a freelance writer this year" is too loose. "I will acquire five writing clients by July 31st" makes it easier to visualize and achieve what you desire.

Measurable: To achieve your goals, you must measure your progress. Establishing clear parameters and identifying interim performance objectives is the only way to know whether you're on or off track. For example, "consistently write blog posts" is not measurable. What does "consistently" mean in this context? You need to have concrete metrics in place, such as "publish one blog post every week," when establishing goals.

Attainable: It feels good to set lofty, ambitious goals—and you *should* aim to set a goal that pushes and stretches you to achieve higher performance. But if you aim too high, you may quickly get off track, become disheartened at your lack of progress, and give up altogether. That's a common occurrence when it comes to goal-setting. The objective isn't to radically transform overnight. It's to rack up small wins that build momentum and motivate you to push forward.

Realistic: You're no doubt a busy person. You may still be busy practicing law. You may have a young child or an elderly relative to care for at home. In an ideal world, you'd have all the time in the world to make uninterrupted progress on your goals. But, of course, you live in the real world, not an ideal one, so make sure your goal-setting conforms with reality. You can do almost anything, just not all at once.

Time-Bound: Time flies when you're having fun, and also when you set out to achieve lofty goals. If you're like most people, you may find yourself setting the same goals year after year because you made little to no progress during prior ones. Don't let yourself off the hook this time. Set an aggressive but realistic time frame for yourself to achieve your goals. As Napoleon Hill once said, "A goal is a dream with a deadline."

Put simply, when setting goals, you need to state specifically what you will do, by when, and have a means to verify whether you've achieved your objective. Anything less is too ephemeral.

Establish and write down no more than three SMART goals for yourself. Make sure your goals align with the Vision Statement and that you can realistically achieve your goals within a one-year timeframe.

TAKE ACTION

Okay, so you've cast a bold vision about what your future as a freelance writer will be like, and written down goals that map to that vision. Now what? Well, now comes the hard part.

It's time to start taking action.

If you're like most lawyers looking to make the leap to freelance writer, this is the point at which you will feel resistance. This is where imposter syndrome really starts to rear its head. It's the crux moment—the hardest part of the climb.

As we discussed in Chapter 2, it's natural and understandable to be fearful of making a big change. Thinking about making change is easy. Moving forward is hard. The good news: If you're feeling fear and resistance, it probably means you're on the right track.

As Steven Pressfield writes in *The War of Art*: "Are you paralyzed with fear? That's a good sign. Fear is good. Like self-doubt, fear is an indicator. Fear tells us what we have to do. Remember one rule of thumb: the more scared we are of a work or calling, the more sure we can be that we have to do it."

The antidote to fear is action, no matter how small or insignificant. Don't place too much pressure on yourself. Don't rush headlong to the destination you seek—try to enjoy the journey. When resistance creeps in, remind yourself that it's not all the big, bold things we do during our lives and careers that lead to success. It's the small actions taken every day that make all the difference and lead to compounding results over time.

Author and marketing guru Seth Godin wrote on his blog: "The thing is, incremental daily progress (negative or positive) is what actually causes transformation. A figurative drip, drip, drip. Showing up, every single day, gaining in strength, organizing for the long haul, building connection, laying track—this subtle but difficult work is how culture changes."

It's how people change, too—including you, if you're committed.

In the following chapters, we'll dive deeper into the actions necessary to help you accomplish your goals.

FOUR

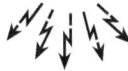

Pick Your Writing Niche

———

I n my adopted hometown of Traverse City, we swim in Lake Michigan in the summer and hit the slopes in the winter. If I want to keep my beer cold at the beach, I buy Yeti. If I want to keep my body warm while skiing, I buy North Face. I don't shop around for the lowest-price cooler or jacket. I invest in the best product that I know is going to solve my issue, and I'll pay the premium price the brand commands. The investment is worth it. I've made the mistake of opting for the low-price generic brand. In most cases, you get what you pay for.

Across all categories of product and service offerings, there are continuums of premium brands and commodity ones. Those in the premium category narrow their positioning (i.e., the articulation of their value proposition) to the point that there are few, if any, available alternatives to what they offer. They solve discrete problems and do it well. Assuming there is a market for what they offer, and their product or service is of high quality, they dominate and earn healthy profits.

You may have observed this dynamic at work In the context of selling legal services. The smartest lawyers aren't necessarily the most successful ones—at least as measured by income. The highest-paid lawyers tend to be those who narrowly focus their practices in order to reduce or eliminate the competition. A lawyer who offers one area of practice expertise for one industry will be perceived as a more valuable resource to those in the industry than another lawyer who purports to specialize in almost everything for everyone. The generalist may get an opportunity (if you can call it that) to participate in an RFP designed to identify the lowest-cost provider for commodity work, while the specialist will get an urgent phone call when it really matters.

The same principles apply when it comes to building a freelance writing business. Establishing a narrow niche is important because it allows you to position yourself as an industry expert to your target audience. Jack- and Jill-of-all-trades generalist writers have trouble gaining traction because, while they may be relevant to almost everyone, they are not seen as an invaluable, must-have resource to anyone. The more you immerse yourself in one industry, versus trying to serve a multitude of different market verticals, the more expertise you'll develop—and the more expertise you develop, the more valuable you'll become.

From marketing copy to thought-leadership articles, having a niche focus helps writers craft more interesting prose. When you deal with the same types of clients with the same types of issues, you start to see patterns and make connections that others can't see. Instead of being stuck at the surface level, you can dig deeper.

In short, narrow niches work because they help position you as an industry expert to your target audience, and the number one thing a writing client wants to know is whether you have expertise in their domain. Without such expertise, the client will doubt whether you're capable of understanding and writing clear, concise and interesting copy about the key issues at play in their industry. As an expert who specializes in writing for a particular industry, you will stand out as the obvious choice—or one of a small cohort of other experts under consideration—for new projects.

The reasons most freelance writers, lawyers and other professionals resist narrowing their focus are twofold. First, they're fearful of missing out on opportunities. Second, they think it will be boring to do the same types of projects for the same types of clients, over and over.

The truth is, you *will* miss out on opportunities when you narrow your positioning as a writer. And that's a good thing! Not every opportunity is one worth pursuing. In fact, most aren't. There are multitudes of "shiny new projects" and poor-fit clients in the writing world that will distract you from your objective to become a well-paid writer doing interesting work. If you don't maintain your focus, you'll tend to view each opportunity as more-or-less equivalent and never gain traction.

As David C. Baker, a leading consultant to creative agencies, writes in his book *The Business of Expertise*: "Positioning is an exercise in irrelevance. As you become more irrelevant to prospects by turning your positioning away from them, you become even more relevant to your chosen target. It requires courage and discipline."

When you clearly communicate to the marketplace what you do best, and who you do it for, you attract quality clients and repel bad ones. Clients who value expertise are willing to pay more. Those who are willing to hire generalists are concerned primarily with obtaining the lowest price possible. The purpose of having narrow positioning is to reduce or eliminate your competition. If you serve a single viable market, you'll be viewed as less interchangeable. There will be high demand for your services. If there is excess supply in your market—and if you're a generalist writer, there will be—you'll continually get beaten up on price. It's basic economics.

As a specialist with a narrow focus, you have more leverage when pricing your services and setting the terms of an engagement. Instead of prospecting, the specialist is presented with opportunities that aren't subject to a competitive process. A specialist can sift through them to identify the right fit. Among the hallmarks of expertise is selectiveness, whereas the generalist has a tendency to chase every opportunity.

As far as wanting to do varied work for a diverse set of clients, let me ask you this: Do you desire variety more than money? Money, of course, isn't everything, but it's the fuel that will allow you to enjoy the flexibility that freelance writing affords. Narrowly focused writers, like specialized lawyers and surgeons, earn higher fees. There are riches in the niches.

It's also highly satisfying and intellectually stimulating to become an expert in a particular field. If you summon the courage to stay in a single lane, you'll come to know what it's like to operate at a high level of competence as a freelance writer, and you won't want to go back to the feelings of uncertainty and angst that afflict the generalists who often get in over their heads. There's a compounding return on expertise. When you're disciplined enough to maintain your focus, you get better and faster at a rate that's impossible for a generalist to keep up with. When you immerse yourself in a particular subject matter, you start to see things others can't. As a result, your writing gets more interesting, and you become more interested in your craft as well.

To summarize, here are some of the most important benefits of having a niche focus:

- **Better Client Relationships:** When you target a niche market with a specific type of client, you can focus on the quality of client engagements and on nurturing your relationships. Your clients share common interests, work within similar organizational structures, and have similar expectations. You can model your business practices (how you manage projects, engage in marketing, bill for your services, etc.) in a way that meets their needs.

- **Greater Visibility:** One of the primary benefits of a niche focus is that it allows you to position yourself as a big fish in a small pond. When you set out to serve everyone, it's nearly impossible to establish an online presence. On the other hand, when you're focused, you can identify where your ideal clients spend their time and attention online, and inject yourself into the conversations happening in their industry. You can become a trusted insider, rather than an outsider who is held at arm's length.

- **Referrals and Word-of-Mouth Marketing:** People

in a niche tend to talk to others in that niche, which means more opportunities to get the word out about your services. For example, lawyers attend bar association events where they spend time speaking with other lawyers, often discussing issues related to marketing and business development. I can tell you from experience that lawyers struggle to find writers to help with projects such as writing website copy or thought-leadership articles, so when a lawyer finds someone who knows what they're doing, they tell the others.

• **More Done in Less Time:** If you write for one type of client and gain a deep understanding of their industry, your writing will get faster and better, enabling you to make more money and make a bigger impact. You'll also realize efficiencies in other aspects of your business. Your website can be more simple and straightforward. Your marketing will become more dialed-in because you're only targeting one audience, and you can develop systems and processes—from billing to client status reports—that meet the needs and expectations of your similarly situated clients.

HOW TO PICK A NICHE

Perhaps you're now open to the idea of narrowing your focus as a freelance writer, but unsure of how to carve out a niche. Let's dive into that.

First, let's more clearly define what a business niche is in the context of freelance writing.

As a writer, a niche involves having a tightly defined service offering for a particular industry. Accordingly, there are two things you need to consider when establishing a niche: what you do, and the types of clients you do it for.

By way of example, consider how a lawyer might go about the process of picking a niche. "Commercial litigator" is not a niche. "Commercial litigator for the automotive industry" is moving in the right direction. "Commercial litigator who exclusively handles UCC disputes for Tier 1 automotive suppliers" is even better. The more you can drill down on a specific service offering for specific clients, the more relevant and attractive you become.

An effective niche is an inch wide and a mile deep. An "inch wide" means that you've clarified your service offering to the point that your target market clearly understands your value proposition. A "mile deep" means that your target market is big enough—there are lots of people looking for the solutions you provide.

When I advise writers (or lawyers) on the best way to go about picking a niche, I encourage them to consider the intersection of their interests, their expertise and marketplace opportunities. So ask yourself three questions:

1. What type of writing do I like to do?
2. What type of specialized expertise do I have or am willing to learn?
3. What opportunities exist in the marketplace? In other words: Are people buying what I'd like to sell?

If you can determine what you like to do, what you're good at, and what market opportunities exist, and then find some commonality among them, you will be on your way to carving out a niche for yourself. However, that's easier said than done. You may find that what "interests" you doesn't always align with the best "market opportunities." For example, you may have an intense interest in a topic

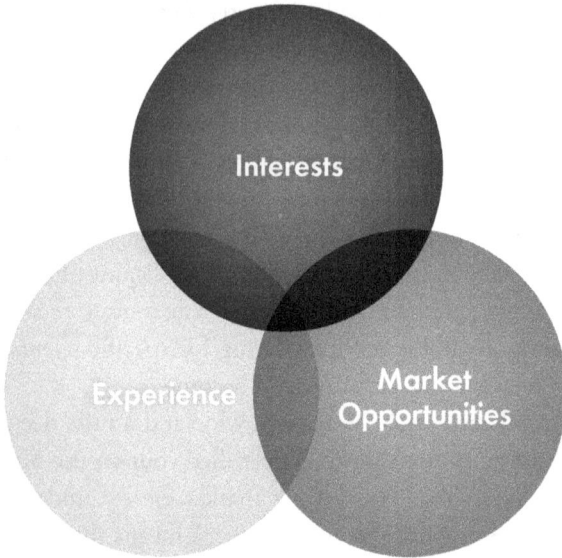

like health and wellness, and be excited about working for clients in the health and wellness industry, but come to find that companies in that space pay low rates since there are so many writers—an oversupply—competing for that work.

"Follow your passion" is not always sound advice, at least if you have bills to pay. Many writers find time to write about what they're passionate about, such as by starting a passion-project blog, only because they've established a freelance niche focused on an industry that offers a profitable market opportunity. This may sound cynical, but one of the best ways to lose passion for something is to spend lots of time pursuing it while living the Spartan lifestyle of a starving artist. Instead of focusing exclusively on your interest in a particular subject matter, remember that, regardless of subject matter, you're looking to create an opportunity to pursue your passion for the craft of writing, itself.

It is also important to keep in mind, especially when

you're just starting your career as a freelance writer, that your narrow focus will reflect the type of work *you pursue,* not necessarily the work *you do.* Until you establish yourself as an expert within a particular industry, it will likely be necessary to take on work outside of your niche as you become known and start generating work within your niche. Again, we all have bills to pay. The goal is to work toward specialization, not put all your eggs in one basket from day one.

When I started writing for clients, I took on almost every project that came my way. At that time, I wasn't really focused on carving out a niche for myself. Writing for so many disparate and varied clients, however, became cumbersome and difficult. I quickly came to the conclusion that if I wanted to build a sustainable writing business, I would need to narrow my focus. I was spending way too much time on individual projects for clients, from hospitals to software companies, across all industries.

Over time, I began honing in on professional services as my sweet spot. But even that wasn't narrow enough. "Professional services" is such a big space that it was hard to wrap my arms and mind around it. There was no way I could become a subject matter expert, or even mildly competent, in the wide range of issues across the spectrum of professional services.

Ultimately, I came to the conclusion that I could make the biggest impact and achieve the greatest success if I focused my attention on the area that aligned with my interests and experience, and presented a significant market opportunity: the legal industry.

I began directing my own marketing exclusively to law firms. I got involved in the Legal Marketing Association. I spread the word among my network of law school classmates and former colleagues. It didn't happen overnight, but over time more of my work began flowing in from law firm clients, most of whom appreciated working with a writer who understood the ins and outs of their industry—how marketing works, and how new business is generated.

As I started gaining traction within the legal industry, I worked on a wide variety of projects, from website and brochure copy for law firms to thought-leadership articles for individual attorneys. As time went on, I transitioned away from writing marketing copy and went all-in on thought leadership. Helping lawyers write and publish thought-leadership content dealing with trending legal issues was more interesting and more lucrative than working on marketing copy. Eventually, I went from being a freelancer to an entrepreneur. Today, I own a public relations and marketing agency that serves law firms across the country, and have a team of writers who work alongside me. That didn't happen all at once. It took years of effort and, most importantly, disciplined focus on my market niche.

All of this is to say that developing a niche focus is not an event—it's an evolution over time. Think of your niche as your North Star. As you begin your journey as a writer, and choose a niche focus, there will be occasions where you stray from it. But never lose sight of it because it's your beacon on your path to greater success. At some point, you may decide to pivot from one area of focus to another. That's fine, but only do so after testing and measuring your results.

Don't be too hard on yourself if you have a hard time narrowing your focus right out of the gate. You may need to spend some time immersing yourself in your new field—at least dipping your toe in the water—before you're able to commit to a direction. Just keep in mind that investing in a niche, like investing for retirement, is a long-term proposition. The results compound over time, not all at once.

You have to remain disciplined and stay the course. If you bounce around too much, you'll never gain traction.

SHOULD YOU WRITE FOR THE LEGAL INDUSTRY?

While the underlying principles of this book are broadly applicable and relevant to anyone who is interested in becoming a freelance writer, it was written for a specific audience: lawyers who want to explore an alternative career path. Since a critical component of picking a niche focus is drawing upon one's experience and expertise, it's natural that you may be considering carving out a writing career focused on serving the legal industry.

Only you can make that decision, but I can help you consider the pros and cons of writing for the industry you're contemplating exiting.

One of the primary benefits of writing for law firms is that the demand for content, and thought-leadership content in particular, is growing. The COVID-19 crisis accelerated many trends that were already in place, and one of the most important trends is an increasing recognition of the important role thought-leadership content plays in legal marketing and business development.

Law firms and lawyers have come around to the idea that one of the only ways to reach people at scale is by creating valuable thought-leadership content. Lawyers can't be everywhere, all at once, but their ideas can be. When a prospective client reads something a lawyer has written that addresses a problem and offers a helpful solution, the client is naturally inclined to think of the lawyer as the right expert to execute the solution. Thought-leadership content allows lawyers to gain awareness and build trust with their audience, and awareness and trust are the precursors to business development.

Law firms have always focused, to one degree or another, on thought leadership. But the COVID-19 pandemic has forced them to double down on it, and that's not likely to change. Again, it was a trend that existed before the world went into lockdown, and it's now accelerating. Most law firms maintain at least one blog, and many have ten or more, and they need to keep them stocked with fresh content.

The problems most law firms and lawyers face when it comes to thought-leadership marketing are twofold: (1) lack of time and (2) lack of effectiveness. As you know, most lawyers are very busy and find it difficult to do any forms of marketing and business development, let alone spending four non-billable hours writing a 1,500-word article. Plus, despite being competent writers, lawyers often can't translate their ability to write an effective legal brief into writing an effective thought-leadership article. Writing for an entrepreneur, an HR executive, or even a general counsel is far different than writing a brief for a judge. Accordingly, many firms look to freelance writers, particularly those who formerly practiced law, to help fill in the gaps.

Because there is high demand for writers who can help law firms keep up with their content marketing, writers serving this market can make a good living—equal to if not in excess of what they earned as a practicing lawyer. The economic calculus for law firms is pretty simple: If a lawyer has a billable rate of $350 per hour, and he or she has plenty of work to do, it's more beneficial for the firm to outsource writing to a freelancer who charges $100 or even $150 per hour, than it is to have the lawyer stop billing. Law firms routinely take advantage of this obvious arbitrage opportunity to get the high-quality content they need at a cost they'll gladly incur because it allows their lawyers to keep bringing in revenue.

Finally, you may decide to serve law firms as a freelance writer in order to stay immersed in the legal industry. I didn't necessarily enjoy practicing law, but there were aspects of the job, such as writing, that I enjoyed more than others. For me, and perhaps you, too, there was nothing more rewarding about the practice of law than crafting a crisp, well-reasoned pleading. As a freelance writer for law firms, you get the opportunity to continue tussling with complex topics through your writing, without the pressures associated with the practice of law. An editor may suggest changes to your work, but there will be no adversary poking holes in it.

There are some downsides to writing for law firms, but I believe that they are outweighed by the benefits. The biggest potential downside—and this will likely not surprise you— is that law firms will often throw hot demands your way. When you have a law firm as a writing client, you'll have to deal with urgent requests to write "Client Alerts" when significant court rulings are released and legislation is passed. It's not uncommon to receive projects with 24-hour, or even same-day, turnaround times. One of the biggest allures of a freelance writing career is the freedom it affords, and you have to sacrifice a bit of that freedom if you choose to work for clients in a fast-paced industry such as the legal industry. However, in my experience, that small trade-off is worth it.

There is a reason the legal industry tends to pay higher rates for freelance writers, and availability and responsiveness is a big part of what law firms are paying for. From time to time, you may get a hot project that disrupts your afternoon plans, but the demands on your time will be nothing like they are as a practicing lawyer.

THOUGHT EXERCISES TO HELP YOU NARROW IN ON YOUR NICHE

Before we wrap up this chapter, I want to provide you with a few more ideas and exercises that may help you narrow in on a niche focus. Thinking through the implications of the Interests, Experience, and Market Opportunity Venn diagram on page 54 is a great starting point, but here are some questions to consider that may help you narrow down your options.

1. What type of writing do you enjoy doing?
2. Are you genuinely interested in learning more about the issues concerning a particular industry?
3. Are there writers you admire that you can model yourself after?
4. Can you leverage your past experiences (work, education, personal) to bring new perspectives to a particular industry?
5. What issues are you passionate about?
6. What insights do you have that clients in a particular industry can benefit from?
7. What new skills and knowledge are you motivated to acquire?
8. What relationships do you have within an industry that you can leverage for opportunities?

GAIN INSIGHT AND RECEIVE GUIDANCE

Choosing an area of focus for your writing business is not easy. It takes courage, creativity, and market insight. And it's one of the key issues I help aspiring writers work through in the OutLaw Writer Academy, a virtual workshop in which I guide OutLaw writers through the process of starting and growing their businesses. If you're interested in accelerating your progress and putting the principles from this book into practice, visit www.outlawwriter.com.

FIVE

Build Your
Personal Brand

———

You've heard the grim statistics: A significant percentage of small businesses fail within their first few years. One of the reasons businesses fail is that, despite earning revenue, they can't dig out of the hole they put themselves in when they started by taking on too much debt. A restaurant or a bakery, for example, can easily cost $1 million to start. Many entrepreneurs who take on too much debt are fighting an uphill battle from day one. Some businesses, such as those who raise venture capital, are forced to part with a significant ownership stake before acquiring a single customer or earning a dollar in revenue.

One of the great things about being a freelance writer is that there are virtually no startup costs. In fact, you probably already have all the tools you need to get started: a laptop and Wifi connection. You can run lean as a writer.

While there is not much you need to buy, there is something you need to build in order to achieve success: your personal brand.

WHAT IS A PERSONAL BRAND?

I don't like the term "personal branding," but it's the best shorthand available to describe the process of positioning oneself for success within a particular market. "Reputation" and "personal brand" are often used synonymously, but they're not the same thing. Reputation is more of an *ex post facto* measure of the personal branding work you've done.

In the context of freelance writing, building your personal brand requires a concerted and strategic effort to describe, position, and promote how your skills and experience are relevant and valuable to those you serve. It's not just about letting your reputation speak for itself. It involves purposefully injecting your unique value proposition into the marketplace.

Whether you're a writer, a lawyer or an electrician, your personal brand is what speaks for you when you're not there to speak for yourself. Jeff Bezos has described a brand as: "What other people say about you when you're not in the room."

Developing a personal brand doesn't happen overnight. It's a lifelong process. There is no single blueprint to follow to build one's personal brand, but strong personal brands share certain characteristics. In particular, they tend to be authentic and consistent. One of the reasons it's important to have a niche focus to your freelance writing business is that it allows you to build a brand with authenticity and consistency—which is nearly impossible if you're bouncing around trying to appeal to multiple markets. You want to be a big fish in a small pond, to be known as the go-to expert writer for a particular market, and your personal brand can help you accomplish that.

There is a reason many corporate brands spend tens of millions of dollars on branding—it works! Branding allows a product or a person to differentiate from competitors. Having a strong brand creates a favorable impression with buyers, and allows them to know what to expect. Setting expectations through branding is critically important. For example, those who buy Apple products do so because they think the products will help them become more unique and creative. Nike has built its brand, and billions of dollars in market capitalization, on the notion that its products will allow people to "do" whatever athletic endeavors they set their mind to. Successful freelance writers establish strong personal brands that similarly enable prospective clients to envision a positive future outcome for themselves.

Before sharing some ideas on how you can build your personal brand as a writer, I want to help you to envision some of the effects of strong branding, including:

More Referrals. When people in your network have a clear understanding of who you help and how you help, you will receive more referrals that are in line with your expertise, and fewer that are not.

More Inbound Opportunities. As with referral sources, clients and prospective clients will have a better handle on what you do best. You will be more discoverable than your undifferentiated competitors. As a result, you will get more inbound opportunities for new writing projects. You won't have to work nearly as hard doing outbound marketing and sales.

More Visibility. Assuming that you're focused on building your brand within a niche market, you will be much more visible to those you hope to serve. The marketing you do—from creating content to networking conversations—will be more relevant and memorable because it will be contextualized for a particular audience.

More Profits. One of the key factors that drives down prices is the availability of alternatives. As a well-branded expert writer, you will reduce competition, and as a result you will command higher fees for your work.

HOW TO BUILD A STRONG PERSONAL BRAND

As a new freelance writer, there are a number of steps you can and should take to build a strong personal brand. But make no mistake, branding is not a one-time event. Your brand has the potential to change every day—for better or for worse—so you need to be constantly vigilant about the signals you're sending to clients, prospective clients and referral sources.

Every touchpoint you have with a client as a freelance writer makes an impression. When you send a proposal, is it clear, concise and free of errors? If there is a typo in your proposal, can you really blame the client for passing on your services?

Having a strong personal brand has always been important. It's even more crucial today, given the shifts that have taken place due to the COVID-19 crisis. Many professionals, including many writers, overlooked the importance of building a personal brand, particularly an online brand, in the past. They relied on their ability to win new business "in the room," through face-to-face interactions. They generated opportunities by prospecting within certain geographic boundaries, taking clients to lunch, and sealing deals with a handshake. Many of these types of old-school marketing tactics are not effective—or even possible—anymore. Today, professionals must focus to a much greater extent on creating awareness and building relationships through digital channels.

COVID-19 did not necessarily cause this change. It merely accelerated change that was already underway. A pre-COVID-19 study conducted by Gartner, a leading B2B research and sales training firm, found that buyers of sophisticated services make it 57 percent of the way through the buying process before they establish contact with an individual service provider. In other words, buyers of services, such as writing, do their due diligence online. They seek out the best person for the job, irrespective of where that person is located.

In order to compete in this environment, a freelance writer must have a strong personal brand that makes them visible and attractive to clients in the digital marketplace of ideas. Without a robust digital footprint, a writer will be virtually invisible to those who rely on Google and social media networks to vet and winnow down their options.

There are a number of personal branding assets you must build in order to succeed.

WEBSITE

—————

I know what you may be thinking: Do I *really* need a website?

I get it. You probably have little technological understanding of what it takes to build a website. It's going to take time, effort and resources to get a website built. And it's just one more thing to take care of on your lengthy to-do list.

I'm all for cutting corners when possible, but you need a website if you're serious about pursuing a freelance writing career.

You can keep it simple. You can do it yourself using a website builder (more on that below). You don't need the world's greatest website. You do, however, need a digital "base camp" to showcase your brand.

Why? There are a multitude of reasons why having a website is important. Here are a few.

First, prospective clients search for writers like you online. A website makes you visible.

Second, your website is the place where you will showcase your portfolio of writing work. Clients want to get a sense of your writing style before hiring you.

Third, having a website helps establish your credibility. Clients can learn more about you and your past experience, and they will feel more comfortable that they are sending their work to a real person with a real business—not some fly-by-night writer looking to make a quick buck.

Fourth, your website can help you increase your efficiency. Many writers (myself included) utilize scheduling tools and intake forms on their websites to help manage new project requests and cut down on back-and-forth email communication.

Tip: I recommend using Squarespace to build your website.

It's what I use. It makes it easy to build a site. There are many templates to choose from. Squarespace sites are easy to manage. There are lots of marketing tools built in. And, perhaps most importantly, you don't really need any technical skills to get a site up and running.

SOCIAL MEDIA

Building your personal brand as a writer requires that you meet new people and develop new relationships. It's possible to do that without social media, but why not take advantage of platforms that have already curated a ready-made audience for you? LinkedIn, for example, has more than 700 million professionals (as of the time of this writing) on its platform. That's a lot of prospective clients and referral sources.

Use social media platforms to make new connections, engage with other people's content, and showcase your writing. The most important social media brand-building tip I can give you is this: Show up. Be consistent. You don't need to—indeed, you shouldn't—spend lots of time on social media that cuts into your writing time. Just a little bit every day will do.

Tip: Don't try to utilize every social media platform. Choose one. If you're focused on a B2B audience, such as lawyers and law firms, get active on LinkedIn. If you're trying to break into the health and fitness space, consider Instagram or Facebook. Go where the audience you hope to serve spends its time and attention.

CLIENT EXPERIENCE

Research suggests that life experiences, not material things, are the key to happiness. Nonetheless, most people still choose to spend more on material items because they perceive them as having greater value.

The same principle applies when it comes to building your personal brand. Provide a service to a client and you'll earn a fee. However, if you provide a positive, memorable client experience, you'll earn a fee plus a loyal ally and enthusiastic advocate for you and your writing business. Clients will come back for more—and bring others along with them.

Accordingly, an important part of building your brand is providing a strong brand experience. The truth is that there will be many other writers out there who can do what you do—and many of them will be better than you at the skill of writing. That's okay. You can set yourself apart by providing a strong brand experience—intangible value that leads to tangible results.

To provide a great experience, consider how you can refine and optimize each touchpoint you have with a client or prospect. From pricing proposals and new client onboarding, to project management and billing, each client interaction is an opportunity to add extra value and cement the relationship.

Tip: When onboarding new clients, I try to subtly unearth information that allows me to add a bit of "surprise and delight" to the relationship. This allows me to do things like send a client a book on a topic I know she's interested in, send a handwritten note before a birthday, or simply inquire about how their child's baseball tournament went. Consider having an established series of questions you ask clients during your onboarding process that allows you to learn information about your client that can be used to provide some surprise and delight of your own.

SOCIAL PROOF

Social proof is a term from psychology that refers to someone's level of perceived credibility. Are you attached to people, brands or institutions that are recognizable and perceived as trustworthy? If so, that affiliation encourages others to perceive you as trustworthy, too.

Common forms of social proof include client testimonials, logos of clients you've worked with, case studies, awards and accolades.

Bolster your personal brand by gathering and showcasing social proof of your experience and expertise as a writer. This information can and should be featured on your website and social media profiles. Naturally, you won't have much social proof to feature when you're just getting started. But as you build your client roster, develop case studies, and publish your writing in prominent publications, let the world know. The trust others show in you will reinforce the decisions of others to trust you as well.

Tip: The best time to ask for a client testimonial is immediately following the completion of a successful writing project. Create a process whereby you ask satisfied clients for a short statement attesting to the quality of your services. You can offer to write a testimonial for the client to review and edit. That often helps to grease the wheels.

SERVE HOW YOU'D LIKE TO BE SERVED

As a practicing lawyer, the importance of client service

has already been drilled into you. Once you're off on your own, running your freelance writing business, take client service to the next level. There's no better way to keep clients happy—clients who will advocate for you—than by going above and beyond on client service in day-to-day interactions with your clients.

Serve your clients the way you would like to be served if you were hiring a professional for an important project. It's the "Golden Rule" of building your personal brand.

Be reliable. Deliver projects on time and on budget. Own up to mistakes and fix them when they happen. Keep the client informed of a project's status. Thank the client for their business. Send notes. Listen intently. Be enthusiastic.

There are thousands of other writers out there competing for the same business. You need to build a brand and reputation that speaks for you when you're not there to speak for yourself.

SIX

Marketing Your Business

—

Every other week, I publish an 800- to 1,200-word blog post on my website related to legal marketing and business development issues. Every month, I write a column on those same types of topics for Attorney at Work and Law.com. I've written three books for lawyers. I host a weekly podcast called The Thought Leadership Project. I frequently speak at state bar association and Legal Marketing Association events. I send out a weekly email newsletter to thousands of lawyers and legal marketers who have signed up to my agency's email list. I post at least one time every day on LinkedIn.

It's a lot of marketing, and a lot of work. Fortunately, after a decade of being in this business, I have a team to help me keep up this pace. I couldn't do it myself.

However, the primary reason I have to engage in so much marketing is that I have a team to support—there are salaries, benefits, and other expenses to pay. I need to have a significant amount of work flowing in to keep everything running.

Some good news: As a freelance writer who is just getting started, you don't have to do nearly as much work to generate income for yourself. But make no mistake—you will have to market yourself and your services. Generating demand for your services through marketing is the lifeblood of your business. You can't sit back and wait for clients to find you. You need to inject yourself into the marketplace of ideas in order to create awareness and build trust with those you hope to serve.

Some more good news: Marketing doesn't need to be complicated. Keep it simple. Make it easy on yourself. Do something you enjoy because then you'll do more of it. Don't overcomplicate things.

It's just like with exercise: Why get on the treadmill if you hate it, especially if you love playing tennis? Both have the potential to get you in shape. But you'll be excited to hit the tennis court, and it won't even feel like exercise. It will be fun. It works the same way with marketing.

Presumably, you're interested in starting a freelance writing business because you enjoy writing. That's great, because the best way to market a freelance writing business is, you guessed it: writing.

By writing and publishing your own content, you're giving your prospective clients a taste of what they will be buying from you. Ever been to Costco? There is a reason they give away so many free samples of their products. People may think they're going to Costco for the free samples, but the odds are they're going home with a cart full of products they purchased.

The best marketing tactic is the one that feels effortless to you. Since writers write, let's focus on a marketing strategy, with writing at its core, that will help you to establish a steady flow of inbound writing requests—no uncomfortable cold calls or awkward networking events required.

CREATE A DIGITAL BREADCRUMB TRAIL

The cornerstones of marketing and business development for any professional service, such as freelance writing, are awareness and trust. Your prospective clients must first become aware of you and the services you provide. Then they must come to trust that you're the right person for the job. A writing-centric marketing approach will help you achieve both objectives.

A key part of generating awareness is meeting your clients where they are. You must get yourself and your brand in front of those you hope to serve in places where they spend their time and attention. This is a fundamental precept of marketing across all sectors of the economy.

For example, one of the reasons companies such as Apple, Nike and Amazon are so successful is that their brands are ubiquitous. They inject themselves into platforms, channels and conversations across the spectrum of communications. They use traditional advertising, social media promotion, content marketing, public relations and other marketing tactics to reach wide audiences. In other words, they use a multichannel approach to marketing.

As a result, when consumers need a phone, athletic shoes or, in the case of Amazon, almost anything, these brands are top-of-mind as the obvious choice. Of course, they need to make and sell quality products, but once they've checked that box, their growth is driven by brand awareness and affinity.

Consider, on the other hand, what would happen if those brands merely relied on a website to inform consumers about their products. It's not much of a leap to surmise that they wouldn't have much success with that strategy. No brand can sit back and expect consumer demand to show up. They must reach people where they are—and today they're spending time seeking information and entertainment on digital channels such as Google, YouTube and social media.

As we addressed in Chapter 4, every writer is a brand, too. Yet many writers seem to believe that it's enough to create a website and wait for the business to start rolling in. A website is important and you should have one. But your website will almost always be the end, not the beginning, of your buyer's journey.

Relying on people to find you and your website amid the junkyard of the Internet will virtually guarantee your anonymity. Prospective clients aren't online searching for a writer's website. They're seeking out answers. They're looking for solutions. They're searching for a story that resonates.

To be visible to those prospects, writers must, like Apple, Nike and Amazon, adopt a multichannel approach to marketing online.

To most of your prospects, the Internet is one big website, and Google and social media are its two primary filters. When someone has a question or needs a recommendation, they rely on two resources: Google's search box and their friends' opinions on social media.

Those are the places that people are spending their time and attention. Your job is to provide them with a trail of breadcrumbs that leads them back to your website and, ultimately, to a new engagement.

The breadcrumbs should consist of articles, blog posts, videos, podcasts or other forms of thought-leadership content you create and publish online. Ideally, you'll publish most of your content on platforms other than your own website—in other words, the places where your target audience consumes information. Every article you write and publish is a breadcrumb. The posts you share on social media are also breadcrumbs.

Done right, each breadcrumb leads to another. For example, you should include links to other thought leadership you've created in every article you write. Your byline in guest posts should link back to your website. Everything you publish in the marketplace of ideas should lead prospects further down the trail.

Here's an example from my own experience to provide some context. My writing audience—lawyers and legal marketers—is pretty defined. And I know what websites they visit for legal marketing and business development ideas and inspiration. I publish on those websites, such as Attorney at Work and Law.com, frequently. Even among the narrowly defined audiences of such websites, I know my content is not for everyone. But a certain percentage of lawyers and legal marketers who traffic those types of websites are interested in the mix of topics, including thought leadership and content marketing, that I typically address.

Some number of the readers of each article I write will click on one of the internal links I've included (leading them to another article on my blog), or check out my website or one of my books via the links in my byline at the end of my articles. After pinballing around the Internet, some people will end up checking out my website bio and LinkedIn profile, listen to my podcast or buy one of my books. They might sign up for my email list. Occasionally one will reach out to discuss business.

See how this works?

If you want to engage your audience online, you can't passively sit by and wait for prospects to stumble upon your website. You need to funnel people in the right direction. You need to be visible, from Google to social media to relevant niche websites, in places where your audience is searching for answers. You need to create a digital path that guides your audience where you want them to go.

In this sense, your website is not your website; it's just one component part. You need to think of your website as your entire body of work spread across the expanse of the Internet.

Ideally, your body of work functions in concert, provoking interest in what you have to say, building trust in your ability to address specific problems, and directing your audience to the final destination of their digital journey: your website and a new engagement.

Now that you have a sense of the big picture of marketing, let's get more specific

TO WORK FOR THOUGHT LEADERS, YOU MUST BECOME ONE

The best way to market your writing business is to understand the motivations and desires of your target audience. Once you understand what your audience wants, you can, through your marketing, position yourself as the person to help others achieve their objectives. Marketing generates awareness. It also builds trust.

In almost every industry, especially those in the B2B sector, such as law firms and other professional services firms, business leaders want to be perceived as thought leaders. They want to make their expertise visible to the world—after all, they're competing in the same digital environment you are.

A "thought leader" is an industry expert who shares his or her expertise with their target audience for the purpose of educating them and adding value. The best thought leaders, like the best business leaders, have a clear point of view and are selfless. They share their ideas and insights because they feel compelled to do so. Their desire to make an impact and foster change results in them casting a vision of the future that others follow.

A delightful consequence of creating and publishing thought-leadership content is that it often redounds to the benefit of the thought leader in the form of new business.

The problem that professionals face is that, despite the obvious benefits of becoming a thought leader, they often don't have the time or the skills necessary to translate their expertise into polished thought-leadership content. And therein lies the opportunity for writers like you.

No matter what industry niche you focus on, almost every business leader in that niche desires to have their expert insights published in the form of thought-leadership articles. Sure, some of that desire may be ego-driven, but there are strong business reasons for business leaders to want to publish as well.

According to the 2019 Edelman-LinkedIn B2B Thought

Leadership Impact Study, 55 percent of B2B decision makers use thought leadership "as an important way to vet businesses they're considering working with."

This finding makes sense in light of the previously mentioned study by Gartner which found that buyers of sophisticated services make it 57 percent of the way through the buying process before they establish contact with an individual service provider.

In other words, buyers are searching for signals of expertise amid all of the noise online, and making buying decisions based on what they find. Without a robust online portfolio of thought-leadership content, a business or business leader is virtually invisible to their customers or clients.

As a writer hoping to serve businesses and business leaders, a key element of your marketing strategy should be establishing yourself as a thought leader for those who hope to become thought leaders themselves.

This is important for two principal reasons.

First, by educating members of your target audience on the importance of writing thought-leadership content, you will generate demand for your services. As a freelance writer whose value proposition is that you can help your clients grow their businesses through the writing you do, it's important to keep in mind that your competitors are not only other writers—you're also competing against all of the other marketers out there extolling the virtues of their own marketing specialities, such as advertising and events. Your clients have many alternatives to the expertise you offer. You must work to reduce or eliminate the competition by educating your prospective clients on the benefits of thought-leadership marketing.

In doing so, you should give away your best ideas for free. Don't hold back. By giving away your best ideas for free in the marketplace of ideas, you'll build an audience of engaged and loyal followers. You'll inspire others to want to become thought leaders—but most won't try to do it themselves. They'll look to you, the person who showed them the way, for assistance.

Second, your thought-leadership writing will demonstrate your writing chops. Some prospective clients—lawyers, in particular—will be skeptical that someone else can write on their behalf. They are going to want to "try before they buy," and samples of your own thought-leadership content can provide the assurance they need to engage your services.

There are many things you can do to market your writing services. But the simple, scalable, inexpensive and effective marketing system described below has served me and many other writers well—and it can benefit you as well. Here are the four steps:

1. Write thought-leadership content for your narrowly defined audience.
2. Publish as much of your content as possible on third-party websites your audience knows, likes and trusts.
3. Build an email list by offering a valuable free download on your website.
4. Promote your content through an email newsletter and on social media.

WRITE THOUGHT-LEADERSHIP CONTENT FOR YOUR NARROWLY DEFINED AUDIENCE

To influence those you hope to serve, you must make

your expertise visible. Unless expertise can be validated through referral or reputation, it must be demonstrated through thought leadership expressed in the marketplace of ideas.

In his book *Good to Great*, Jim Collins introduced the concept of the "Flywheel Effect," which describes the increasing momentum that companies gain when they land on an effective process for producing, marketing and selling products or services. It takes a great deal of effort to turn the flywheel at the beginning, but then it picks up speed and continues to reinforce a business's advantage. According to Collins, "Each turn of the flywheel builds upon work done earlier, compounding your investment of effort."

There's a flywheel effect to thought leadership as well. When a freelance writer starts producing thought-leadership content for a narrowly focused audience, the process forces her to crystallize her thinking. Her thought leadership attracts the attention of prospective clients, some of whom will hire her to write for them. Through the writing work she does for those clients, she deepens her expertise and sharpens her skills. As a result of her experience, she is then able to produce more insightful thought leadership. And so on. The flywheel turns faster and faster.

Thought Leadership Flywheel

Engagement

Awareness and Trust

AUTHORITY

Expertise

Thought Leadership

The best way to get the thought-leadership flywheel turning is to resist the urge to write for the masses. Instead, when writing your own thought-leadership content, tailor it to your narrowly focused audience. In fact, have a specific person with a specific job title in mind and address their needs. Write like you'd speak to them. Fight your instinctive belief that the best way to reach a big audience is to write something that is broadly relevant. Trust that a narrowly focused article that is hyper relevant to a small constituency will make a more significant impact (on your reader, and on your business).

For instance, when I'm writing thought-leadership content to promote my business, I write it for lawyers. But not all lawyers. I primarily work with lawyers who have practices serving businesses, not consumers, so that informs how I craft my own content. I want my message to be highly relevant to members of my audience and demonstrate my understanding of their businesses. Among all the other writers out there, I want to make sure that I resonate with my audience: lawyers, typically at midsize to large law firms, who have B2B practices.

It would be easy to make my content more broadly relevant to a bigger audience. After all, the way lawyers market themselves is virtually the same as the way consultants, accountants and other professional services providers do. But by making my content more relevant to more people, I'd necessarily have to make it more generic and watered down. As a result, I might have more followers, but fewer fans. Followers browse. Fans buy.

This is the reason that Seth Godin urges us to pursue the "minimum viable market" when marketing our services. He writes:

"When you seek to engage with everyone, you rarely delight

anyone. And if you're not the irreplaceable, essential, one-of-a-kind changemaker, you never get a chance to engage with the market.

The solution is simple but counterintuitive: Stake out the smallest market you can imagine. The smallest market that can sustain you, the smallest market you can adequately serve. This goes against everything you learned in capitalism school, but in fact, it's the simplest way to matter.

When you have your eyes firmly focused on the minimum viable audience, you will double down on all the changes you seek to make. Your quality, your story and your impact will all get better.

And then, ironically enough, the word will spread."

People want to read content that seems like it was written specifically for them. If you have a clearly defined audience, it will be far easier to craft and contextualize content that stands out.

A good way to get started is to consider what I like to call the Focusing Question: What does my ideal client need to know, understand or believe before they will do business with me?

The objective is not to sell through your content by overtly pitching your services, but rather to address—with laser focus—the questions, challenges and opportunities that your audience is grappling with. When you address these issues through your thought-leadership writing, your audience will come to the logical conclusion that you're the right writer for the job.

PUBLISH CONTENT ON THIRD-PARTY WEBSITES YOUR AUDIENCE KNOWS, LIKES AND TRUSTS

If you have a website for your writing business, your instinct will be to publish as much of the content you write as possible on your own platform. After all, you will want Google to rank your site in search results and visitors to have a positive experience when they visit your site, and having lots of content on your site can help accomplish both objectives.

But there is a better way: publishing most of your content off-site on third-party platforms. Executives, entrepreneurs, lawyers and other consumers of marketing content are busy. When they spend time online, they're visiting sites they already know, like and trust—and yours (and mine) are likely not among them.

By understanding where members of your target market consume their information, you can seek to publish your thought-leadership content there. By having your byline and a link back to your website appear on a high-traffic platform that the audience you are trying to reach already trusts, you can leverage the credibility the platform already has with its audience, thereby helping you to build trust with new audience members.

As we discussed previously, the content you share on such platforms creates a digital breadcrumb trail back to your own website. In addition, by including a link back to your writing website, you'll increase the chances that your website will start ranking more highly in Google search results.

SEO is a tricky topic. Google doesn't spell out the exact formula for getting a site to rank. However, Google has made clear that earning backlinks from high quality websites is one of the most important factors in improving SEO performance. If high "domain authority" websites are linking to content on your website, that's a strong indicator to Google that your website contains information worth ranking. Accordingly, not only does guest posting get your thought leadership in front of a wider audience, it also helps immensely with SEO.

Here are three tips to get you started with guest posting.

1. **Find the Right Platforms.** Start by asking yourself: What is the go-to platform where my target audience consumes content? This doesn't mean that you should necessarily be looking for the platform with the biggest audience. It would be great to publish something in *The Wall Street Journal*, but a smaller platform that is geared directly to your niche audience may be just as, if not more, effective to showcase your expertise.

2. **Pitch an Original Idea.** If you want the editor of a site with high standards to pay attention to your pitch, then you need to come up with an original idea. Do your research. Take note of the types of content and topics that are popular on the site you're pitching. Monitor the news and stay on top of issues trending in the industry you're focused on. It's not easy to get past the gatekeepers—but it's easier than it used to be. There are more outlets than ever to publish on, and the media and publishing industries have been particularly hard hit by the economic fallout from COVID-19. Platforms are being forced to do more with less, and that means you have the opportunity to help editors do their jobs (i.e., fill their websites with content that gets clicks), and earn yourself exposure as a result.

3. **Create High-Quality Content.** This should go without saying, but if you're writing for an authoritative site you need to bring your "A" game and cre-

ate great content. Write with the platform's audience in mind. Don't hold anything back for fear of giving away the special sauce. Cite authoritative sources and use research data to buttress your points.

4. **Republish the Content on Your Website.** The idea of pursuing an outside publishing strategy gives some writers pause. They worry that by publishing on other platforms, there will be a dearth of content on their own websites. However, most third-party platforms don't insist on owning the copyright when you write for them. While you may be restricted from publishing the content with another outside platform, you can almost always post it on your own website. Always check the guidelines, but rarely do you have to relinquish the copyright to your work when publishing elsewhere.

The more you pitch your content to third-party gate-keepers, the more effective you will be doing so on behalf of your clients. The more editorial relationships you develop, the greater the likelihood that you can leverage those relationships in the future. The flywheel keeps turning.

BUILD AN EMAIL LIST BY OFFERING A VALUABLE FREE DOWNLOAD ON YOUR WEBSITE

One of the primary objectives of writing thought-leadership content is to drive prospective clients to your website. Ideally, after being inspired by the ideas you share through your content, a website visitor will reach out to hire you to write for them. But that scenario is the exception not the rule.

In most cases, those who read your content and visit your website will be intrigued but not immediately ready to buy. More trust will need to be established, the timing will not be right, or both.

For these types of website visitors—browsers but not yet buyers—you need to offer an opportunity for them to stay engaged with you, but on their terms. This is accomplished by creating a "transitional call to action."

A "call to action" on a website—a "buy" button on a B2C website or a "contact" button on a B2B one—is for those who are ready to act. A transitional call to action, on the other hand, recognizes that many visitors may need more time to evaluate an offering. It gives them the opportunity to stay in touch, learn more about you, and take action when a need arises.

A transitional call to action offers your visitors something valuable, called a "lead magnet," that they can download on your website in exchange for their email address. A lead magnet can be something as simple as the opportunity to subscribe to your blog or as substantive as a free ebook. The more valuable the lead magnet is to your audience, the more email addresses you will collect.

The email address goes directly into an email service provider (such as MailChimp) so that you can continue the conversation by sending them valuable information over time via email. When an email subscriber is ready to take action, you'll be top of mind because you'll be at the top of their inbox on a consistent basis.

If you'd like to see a few examples of lead magnets that have generated thousands of email subscribers for my business, visit the "Free Resources" page on my website: www.hcommunications.biz/free-resources.

PROMOTE YOUR CONTENT THROUGH AN EMAIL NEWSLETTER AND ON SOCIAL MEDIA

In *The Field of Dreams*, a voice tells Kevin Costner's character to "build it and they will come." When it comes to writing thought-leadership content, "write it and they will come" is advice that will ensure your obscurity. You must actively market and promote your content via email and across social media for it to make an impact.

Email seems old school, but it's the most valuable marketing tool you have available. When someone opts in to your email list, they have invited you to appear in their email inbox. Unlike most forms of marketing, email marketing ensures that you have a direct line of communication to your audience. It's inexpensive. It's effective. And it's free of gatekeepers (other than spam filters).

If you're creating new content every week, you should send an email newsletter promoting your content and services to your subscribers at least every month. By creating a lead magnet, and consistently collecting email addresses, your email list will grow. Each new contact on your list increases the odds that your email newsletter will generate a return on your investment.

Beyond email, the best place to promote your content is on social media. To be effective on social media, you must choose the right platform. You don't need to be on all the platforms. In fact, I recommend focusing on just one.

Where do members of your target audience spend their time and attention? Where are they looking for information of the variety you're addressing through your content? Since I primarily serve lawyers and law firms, I spend almost all of my time on LinkedIn. I post there every day, often twice a day. And I engage with the content of others in my network. I may tweet from time to time, but almost all of my social-media energy is focused on LinkedIn, which is where lawyers and legal marketing professionals are present and active.

Many people steer clear of social media—they may lurk but not engage—because they don't want to come across as self-promotional. That's a mistake, because social media offers tremendous opportunities, especially for writers.

Self-promotion should not be your objective. Rather, you must approach social media with an abundance mindset. Having an abundance mindset on social media means catalyzing conversations by freely sharing your best ideas, engaging with and sharing other people's content, and bringing positivity to the platform. If you're writing high-quality content, share your abundance of wisdom by sharing your content. And celebrate the work of others.

The more you actively and generously engage on social media, the more the "rule of reciprocation" kicks in. Good things redound to the benefit of those who give of themselves and help others.

GETTING YOUR FIRST WRITING GIGS

You have to start somewhere on your journey to becoming a successful freelance writer. It will take some time for your marketing to start bearing fruit. And it's important to get some paid writing gigs under your belt, even if they're low-paying jobs, in order to build a portfolio that helps you get more work from better clients.

One way to do this is to lean on your friends-and-family

network. You may not be ready to broadcast to the world that you're pursuing a freelance writing career yet (because you're still working as a lawyer), but you can discreetly spread the word among your close contacts. Some of those in your circle may be in a position to utilize your writing skills. You can offer them your friends-and-family discount and it's a win-win for everybody. They get the writing they need and you get experience and work to add to your portfolio.

Another option is to find work on freelance platforms such as Upwork or Fiverr. Relying on these platforms is not a good strategy for the long term. The work tends to pay low rates and you'll be competing with other freelance writers around the world for it. That being said, there are legitimate, well-paying companies searching for freelance talent who use these platforms. You may want to pick up a few gigs as a short-term solution. Doing so will help you gain experience and create writing samples that allow you to land better and more sustainable work down the road.

THE BALANCE BETWEEN MARKETING AND BUSINESS DEVELOPMENT

It's important to keep in mind, when you're just getting started and throughout your career as a freelance writer, that the marketing work you do to promote your business is critically important, but it's not a complete substitute for business development. I like to think of marketing as the branding, writing, advertising, and other communications that are intended to initiate an asynchronous conversation with prospective clients. It's the work you create that speaks for you when you're not there to speak for yourself. Business development, on the other hand, involves synchronous communication—it's having a conversation with a prospective client about a specific problem that you can solve.

Marketing occurs largely across the Internet. As a writer, it's your thought-leadership content, your social media posts, and your monthly email newsletter. Business development is more up close and personal. It happens on the phone and on Zoom calls, at networking events, at coffee shops, and at the client's office.

For many freelance writers who, like me, are introverted, asynchronous marketing that can be done alone from the comfort of a home office is much more appealing than business development. However, if all you do is marketing, it's going to be hard to land new clients, especially at the beginning of your writing career. Until you've built up a significant body of marketing work, your marketing won't have the velocity, by itself, necessary to sustain your business. You will need to pursue direct conversations with clients (i.e., business development) in order to increase your odds of landing work. The good news for fellow introverts out there: the more marketing you do, the more you can rely on that marketing to generate inbound inquiries and high-quality leads moving forward.

GAIN INSIGHT AND RECEIVE GUIDANCE: OUTLAW WRITER ACADEMY

If you're interested in learning the step-by-step process I used to quickly grow a six-figure freelance writing business, consider joining the OutLaw Writer Academy. You will receive the exact marketing blueprint you need to attract and retain ideal-fit clients. If you're interested in accelerating your progress and putting the principles from this book into practice, visit www. outlawwriter.com.

SEVEN

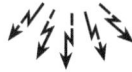

Freelance Writer FAQs

—

I f you're a lawyer considering an alternative career as a writer, you're not alone. How do I know? I get emails and LinkedIn messages every week from lawyers who are at varying points on their writing journeys—from "writer-curious" to professional writer. They perceive me as someone who has gotten over the hump, and they shoot questions my way concerning various issues they're grappling with.

In this chapter, I identify some of the most frequently asked questions I receive from aspiring writers, and provide answers based on my own experiences—the wins and fails. The odds are that if others have struggled with these issues, you may too, so hopefully this will help flatten your learning curve.

LEGAL ISSUES

It should go without saying, but say it I must (and I'm sure you understand why), that my answers to these "legal issues" questions are not and should not be construed as legal advice. You should rely upon your own judgment in determining how to best proceed with respect to these questions and/or consult with an attorney to help you with your particular circumstances.

SHOULD I SET UP A CORPORATE ENTITY FOR MY WRITING BUSINESS?

On the one hand, it's a bit of a pain and there is some expense involved in setting up and maintaining an LLC for a freelance business. On the other hand, it's a relatively simple step that gives you peace of mind that your personal assets are protected (and may provide some potential tax benefits).

Across the risk continuum for all types of businesses, running a freelance writing business lies pretty far toward the low-risk end. However, there are a few pitfalls out there to be aware of. For one, and as you know, whenever two parties enter into a contract for paid services, there is always the possibility that something will go wrong and a dispute will arise. In addition, and more pertinent, there is a risk that you, as the writer, can get embroiled in a dispute between your client and a third party. For example, there are "copyright trolls"—companies who scour the Internet for instances where copyrights they have acquired have allegedly been violated—whose business model is sending demand letters and filing lawsuits in hopes of forcing a quick settlement.

As the writer, there is a risk that you could get dragged into a dispute if your client gets sued. These types of cases typically lack merit, but it's comforting to know that your personal assets are protected on the off chance you and your client get targeted.

SHOULD I HAVE CONTRACTS IN PLACE WITH MY CLIENTS?

I don't use a contract for every engagement, but on balance, it's a good practice to implement. Having an enforceable contract in place will help protect your legal rights (right to payment, payment terms, assignment of copyright, etc.). I trust you've already considered these issues. What you may not have considered is that a contract can also help set the client's expectations for the engagement.

In my experience, the most valuable aspect of having a simple contract in place is that it helps prevent "project creep." Project creep arises when a client starts asking for more than was bargained for.

Let's say a client has hired you to write a thought-leadership article. Once it's done and approved, the client comes back and asks you to write a "quick" summary of the article that they can feature when sharing the article on social media. "I'm sure it will only take you a few minutes," the client says.

Without a contract in place that clearly delineates the scope of the project, you may agree to this supplemental request without further compensation because, you figure, you may not have been clear enough in setting expectations. With a clearly defined agreement to fall back on, all you need to do is point to the contract.

MONEY ISSUES

It may not surprise you to hear that the most frequent of frequently asked-questions I receive from aspiring writers relate to the issue of money. For many, contemplating the leap from salaried lawyer to freelance writer gives rise to all sorts of fears around economic uncertainty and insecurity—some rational and others irrational. Unless you have or had your own book of business as a lawyer, it's likely that you've never been forced to have conversations with clients about pricing, collecting on invoices, and other money issues that can be uncomfortable. As a freelance writer, like it or not, it's a part of the job.

HOW SHOULD I PRICE MY SERVICES?

Pricing writing services is similar to pricing legal services in that you're selling your time, so you need to determine the value of your time. Yes, you will need to determine your hourly rate. No, you won't be a slave to timekeeping the way you are, or were, as a lawyer.

Your hourly rate should be determined based on your skill, experience and the market you serve. And you should be consistently assessing whether you can push it higher. If you're bidding on work and winning a significant percentage of what you bid on, that's likely a sign that your rate is too low. If you're always striking out, your rate may have to come down.

You can research average hourly rates for writers online, but I wouldn't put too much stock in statistical averages. One of the reasons I've been pushing so hard on issues like personal branding and establishing yourself as a thought leader is that most writers don't focus on these things—to their detriment. How you position yourself has a big impact on your perceived value to clients. A freelance writer with a polished website, lots of writing samples, a robust social media presence, and meaningful client testimonials will have a pricing advantage.

Don't sell yourself short by offering a bargain-basement rate, but make sure you understand the reasonable expectations of the market you serve. I advise most aspiring writers to pursue work from companies in B2B industries, such as the legal industry, because they value writing, it's an integral part of their marketing strategies, and as a result, they're willing to pay high rates for it.

While writing this, I took a moment to skim through a number of online articles that surfaced in response to the following Google query: "How much do freelance writers earn for a blog post?" The responses suggest a range between $50 at the low end and $500 at the high end. You can do better. I've been doing this for a while, but within a couple years after I started writing, I was consistently earning in excess of $500 per 1,000 to 1,250 word article. Now I charge between $800 and $1,000.

A $1,000 fee for a great article for a law firm is a bargain. It would likely take a practicing lawyer four hours to write what I can write in two hours. If their hourly rate is $400 per hour, then paying me $800 to do the work should be a no-brainer since the lawyer can generate $1,600 billing clients instead of writing.

You'll want to have a sense of how long it's taking you to write articles for clients, but you won't need to record every six-minute increment of your time. Most clients prefer that you quote them a fixed fee rather than an hourly rate. Rarely will clients ask what your hourly rate is. What they want is upfront clarity about the total cost, and this can work to your benefit. As you get faster and better at what you do, you can turn your $150 per hour rate into a $300 per hour rate. It's certainly within reason to estimate that a writing project for a 1,200-word article will take four hours. If you quote a fixed fee on that basis, and can deliver a quality work product in two hours, you've just doubled your hourly rate.

There's nothing improper or unethical about this. Part of the bargain struck in agreeing to a fixed fee is that the client gets certainty about pricing, and in return you deliver quality writing—regardless of how long it takes. Clients care about the finished product, not the time it took to create it.

WHAT IS THE BEST WAY TO GET PAID: CREDIT CARD, ONLINE PAYMENT SERVICE, DIRECT DEPOSIT CHECK?

There is nothing like watching your bank account grow as the fruits of your writing labor start pouring in. It's the most tangible, objective signal that your hard work is resonating with the marketplace.

But how, exactly, should you request to be paid? There are myriad options, from check to PayPal, at your disposal.

Determining the means by which you get paid is an area in which you should allow your clients' preferences to dictate your approach. One of the questions you should ask clients during your client onboarding process is how they prefer to pay.

Many clients, especially larger organizations, have strict accounts payable policies. Smaller clients tend to be more flexible. So your best approach is to set up various payment options that are likely to meet any client's needs.

Some clients prefer to pay by check. The downside to accepting checks is that it often takes longer for a client to issue a check, and you'll have to spend time to deposit the check, but there will be no transaction fees that eat into your profit margin. One way (that I recommend for all forms of payment) to speed up your cash flow is to request half the project cost upfront and half upon completion. This is not always possible when a project is a "rush job," but it's a good practice to employ.

Other clients will want to pay by credit card. Fortunately, accepting credit card payments online is far easier than it used to be. Most cloud-based bookkeeping systems, like QuickBooks or Xero, allow you to generate invoices with a link to pay by credit card. You will have to set up a credit card processing account with a service like Stripe in order to receive credit card payments, which is a simple and straightforward process.

You can also use a Stripe account to accept credit card payments directly via your website. When you accept a credit card payment, you will be charged a transaction fee of around three percent, so the speed and ease of this form of payment comes at a cost. You may decide to include a surcharge on your invoices—half or the full amount of the credit card processing fee—to offset payments made by credit card.

Another option is to accept payments via direct deposit to your bank account or through an online payment service like PayPal. This is a great way to go for clients you're serving on a consistent basis for a consistent scope of work. For example, I'm on retainer for a number of clients for whom I write an agreed upon number of articles per month on an ongoing basis. Instead of generating an invoice after the work is done, and waiting 30 days for payment, I set up recurring payments via direct deposit or PayPal that allow me to get paid in advance of the work being done.

I'm a big fan of simplifying processes and systems as much as possible. Less is more. But when it comes to how you get paid, more is often better in order to meet the preferences of your clients and structure arrangements that align with the unique circumstances of each engagement. The more options you create, the more quickly and easily you will be able to get money into your account.

HOW MUCH MONEY CAN I REASONABLY EXPECT TO MAKE DURING MY FIRST YEAR AS A FREELANCE WRITER?

This is nearly impossible for me to answer with any specificity. There are so many variables baked into this question. Do you have a portfolio of non-legal writing (as in, not legal briefs or memoranda), such as thought-leadership articles you've written and published that you can use to reinforce that you're a strong writer? Are you serving a market, such as the legal industry, that tends to pay top-of-market rates to writers? Are you treating your writing business as a side hustle, or are you putting full-time effort into it? Are you charging what you're worth? Are you marketing your services aggressively and following the best practices I laid out in prior chapters? These and other factors will play a big role in determining what you earn.

With that being said, and assuming you're being disciplined, strategic, and working full-time in your business, I would say that you can reasonably expect to make $50,000 to $75,000 in your first year. If you're earning $350 per article, write three articles per week, and pick up a few other writing projects, such as copywriting for websites, you will easily fall within that range. Those may seem like some big "ifs" to work through, but you're capable of doing so. Even better: Once you gain some traction with clients, get revenue in the door, and work product out in the world, you'll start getting repeat business and word-of-mouth referrals that will drive your business forward and your income higher in the years to come.

MARKETING ISSUES

You're a lawyer, not a marketer (yet), so it's natural that you may have lots of questions about how to go about marketing your business. In prior chapters, I laid out a simple marketing framework that will help you generate a steady stream of awareness and opportunities. However, you may feel overwhelmed about the process of getting some of your marketing systems in place. If so, you're not alone. Here are some additional tips for getting your marketing engine running on all cylinders.

DO YOU ADVISE HIRING A MARKETING AGENCY TO HELP WITH MY MARKETING?

Yes and no.

Yes: Unless you have a keen eye and some technical

skills, you may want to hire someone to help get your brand off the ground. You don't necessarily need to hire an agency—a couple of freelancers such as a graphic designer and web developer may be all that is necessary to get your logo designed, website built, and email marketing platform up and running. You don't need a world-class brand that an expensive agency might design (or might not), just a brand that "meets spec" in that it presents you in a polished and professional light.

No: You should not rely on an outside vendor to do your ongoing marketing. That's on you. I know, it may seem like a paradox that I'm advising you to position yourself as someone who can help other businesses and professionals market themselves, but suggesting you not engage others to help with your own marketing. But it's important that you embrace the role of marketer for your own business.

You need to get your authentic voice and point of view out into the world. Other people (such as lawyers) hire marketers because they lack the time or skill set, or both, to do it themselves. They believe their time is better spent elsewhere, which is often the case. Don't outsource your marketing, such as your social media activity, to someone else no matter how much you hate the idea of engaging with others on social media. You need to present yourself in the best way possible, and that's by showing up in places where your clients spend their time and attention with your own unique voice.

MINDSET ISSUES

According to Robin Sharma, "The mind is a wonderful servant but a terrible master." Your mind is the asset that will allow you to make the shift to a fulfilling new career, but you'll have to get over a number of mental hurdles along the way.

SHOULD I QUIT MY JOB IMMEDIATELY TO GO FULL-TIME FREELANCE?

This question, again, depends on your individual circumstances, and requires me to throw a few questions back your way. Do you have a family to support? Do you have an income-earning spouse or partner who can cover expenses as you get up and running? What is your appetite for risk? Do you have any clients lined up, such as friends-and-family clients, that you know will send you work? How certain are you that you want to do this?

The more uncertainty you have around these issues, the more sense it makes to start your writing business as a side hustle. Start writing for a few clients on nights or weekends. You'll create some consistent cash flow and get a sense of whether you are, in fact, ready to make the leap.

WILL I BE LONELY WORKING FOR MYSELF?

If you're someone who needs constant stimulus and the energy of an office, then the writer's life may not be for you. Your new office will be wherever you happen to be with your laptop computer.

We have all become accustomed, to one extent of another, with the benefits of working from home. With those benefits also come some drawbacks—one of which is that it can be lonely working by yourself. And when you're off on your own as a freelance writer, as opposed to a work-from-home lawyer whose days are filled with interactions with colleagues and clients, it can feel pretty isolating.

There are steps you can and should take to lessen the loneliness.

- Get out of the house to work somewhere else once in a while. The buzz of a coffee shop can help you get out of your own head.

- Schedule breaks. Don't sit at your desk all day. Get outside and take a walk. Meet up with a friend. Get some exercise. Break up your routine.

- Collaborate on a project. You'll typically be working alone on writing projects for clients. Look for opportunities to work with other writers on a writing project, such as an article on the value of thought-leadership marketing.

- Find an online community. I've found most writers to be collaborative, helpful, and generous people. Find a tribe online consisting of other abundance-minded writers who actively share ideas and provide support and encouragement to one another.

If you'd like to participate in a community of like-minded writers, have access to live training and Q&A sessions, and learn the step-by-step process that will help accelerate your progress as a freelance writer, join the OutLaw Writers Academy. It's a great place to learn and be inspired by other people who are on the same journey as you. To learn more, visit www.outlaw-writers.com.

WHAT IS A TYPICAL DAY LIKE FOR A FREELANCE WRITER?

I don't think there is a "typical" day for writers, so I'll share mine. If there's one commonality to my days, it's that I try to structure them in chunks, with different chunks throughout the day devoted to different priorities. As a writer, it's key to schedule your time in a way that allows you to have at least a couple of long, uninterrupted periods of time to write—for clients and for yourself.

I have three young kids, so over the last ten years I have become a morning person. I wake up around 5 a.m., get a cup of coffee, and sit down at the computer. I write from 5:30 a.m. to 7:30 a.m., while my kids are still sleeping. The early morning writing I do is for me—not my clients. This is the time I write my books and the thought-leadership articles that support the marketing of my business. I consider this to be the most important writing I do all day (and it's the most enjoyable).

After getting the kids up and situated, by 9 a.m. I'm back at my desk ready to shift into client service mode. I spend 15 minutes getting my day planned and creating my to-do list. Since I have employees in my agency, I carve out about 45 minutes to delegate work, discuss projects, and answer questions so everyone is clear about their objectives for the day. I also rely on a few freelancers to help with overflow writing work, so I will also touch base with them, as necessary.

By 10 a.m. or so, I start writing for clients. On a really good day, I'm able to write, edit, and complete two article assignments for clients. More typically, especially if a project is complex and requires research, I will finish one assignment.

I try to wrap up writing by 2 p.m. every day. By that point I've lost steam. Late afternoons are reserved for business development conversations, client coaching calls, interviews with clients for upcoming writing projects, and other miscellaneous tasks. Some days, I will reserve the afternoon for administrative tasks like invoicing, bookkeeping and organizing.

I try to wrap up my workday by 4:30 p.m. If I'm feeling energized, particularly if I'm working on a book, I will try to sneak in an hour more of writing at night.

Throughout the day, I find it important to squeeze in short breaks for exercise or to simply get outside for a few minutes. It's hard to be at the computer all day, so make sure you carve out a bit of time to recharge.

My daily routine is unique to me. Yours will almost certainly be different. What is important is having a routine. One of the challenging (but also delightful) things about being a freelance writer is that you will have nearly complete control of your schedule. Being rigorous and having discipline is what will allow you to get your work done, and also have an interesting and fulfilling life outside of work.

CHAPTER 7

EIGHT

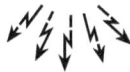

Expanding Your Business

———

I t's not going to be easy to part with the relative financial security of being a practicing lawyer for what you may still perceive as a risky entrepreneurial venture. Many lawyers tend to be risk-averse, which led them to the profession in the first place. A degree in psychology, political science or journalism (my undergraduate major) didn't seem that fruitful, so they made their way to law school. Despite lacking passion for a legal career, practicing law at least seemed like a safe bet in an uncertain world.

After entering the workforce, many lawyers become entrenched, unable to break free because they're bound by golden handcuffs. While earning a good salary as a law firm associate, they're even more enticed by the prospect of the pot of gold waiting for them upon making partner.

These financial factors weighed heavily on my own decision to leave the practice of law. Fears about money (or lack thereof, to be precise) led me to spend quite a few nights lying awake stressing about my future financial prospects as a writer.

One day I woke up and realized that grinding away at a job I was ambivalent about (at best) for the next two to three decades, while missing out on the healthiest and most energetic years of my life, was no way to live. I determined that I was willing to accept the trade-off of greater financial uncertainty to live a life on my terms, with greater autonomy and time to enjoy things I'm passionate about during my prime years—as opposed to my so-called golden years. I didn't want to miss my kids growing up, only to retire at the time when they set off to lead their own lives. So I made the leap.

What I didn't anticipate at that time, but have come to learn over the last decade spent working for myself, is that you don't have to make a financial trade-off to become a writer. There are plenty of opportunities to make a comfortable—even significant—income as a writer. Reject the idea that writers are destined to become starving artists. You can become a thriving entrepreneur.

As I discussed earlier, it's entirely possible to earn a solid six-figure income as a freelance writer. If you're driven, ambitious and smart, you can earn much more than that. Many freelance writers, myself included, develop multiple streams of income that supplement the writing work they do for clients. Typical supplemental income streams for writers include things like consulting, coaching, public speaking, writing books, training and online courses.

As you conceptualize your business, think of your writing as the "wheel" and all of the other ways you monetize your expertise as the "spokes" that attach to the wheel. Over time, a supplemental income stream may become your main source of income.

Even if writing remains at the core of your business, it's still a good idea to have additional, related ways to generate work. If your business, like your investment portfolio, is not diversified, you're subject to more market risk. Situations can change. Budgets can be cut. Even if you have a number of writing clients, if you're providing the same service for everybody, there's more risk involved.

When getting started, I only set out to write, but over the last decade I have developed three additional income streams that collectively exceed the income I generate from writing for clients. These supplemental income streams have a few things in common. One, they all relate to my core area of expertise (legal marketing and business development) for my core audience (lawyers and law firms). Two, they rely on leverage—I earn income from work performed by other people who I pay to provide a service, or products that I create once and sell over time. Three, they are things I enjoy doing, not things I do only for the money.

Writing Books. Writing a book takes a long time, often a year or more. All of the books I've written have been for lawyers, and since I'm writing for such a niche audience, I don't sell massive amounts of books. Since the economics of book pricing and book publishing are such that authors earn only a few dollars per book sold, book sales are not a significant part of my income. But book writing is something

I enjoy doing, and it's an important part of marketing my business. From coaching to consulting, a meaningful percentage of my clients read one of my books before engaging my services.

At some point in your writing journey, you may decide to write a book. Most freelance writers—in fact, most people—harbor a desire to become a published author. An oft-cited statistic from a 2002 *New York Times* article suggests that over 80 percent of people have a book in them waiting to come out. I think writing a book can be a valuable experience, even if you don't sell many copies. But it's not one to be undertaken lightly. It requires a tremendous amount of hard work. In many cases, that hard work can be allocated toward more financially beneficial endeavors. That said, allow me to briefly talk you out of, and then into, the idea.

Don't write a book because:

- It will take a year (unless you're aggregating previously written material). What else can you accomplish in that time?

- You won't sell many copies. The average self-published book sells 250 copies in its lifetime.

- It will be a struggle. You'll think you're done. You'll be sure you've caught all the mistakes. And yet you'll still have a long way to go.

On the other hand, do write a book because:

- It will take a year. At a time when everything we do seems to be speeding up, the book-writing process forces you to slow down and clarify your thoughts.

- You won't sell many copies—but you don't have to. If you're writing a business book, write it for the smallest viable audience. Establish yourself as an authority in a niche.

- It will be a struggle. You'll develop discipline, grit and perseverance in the process. You'll become a better writer, which will benefit everything else you do.

On balance, writing books has been beneficial for my business. Perhaps more importantly, the book-writing process is something I enjoy—I must, because I keep doing it. If you decide to write a book, it doesn't have to be on a topic that relates to your business. But if you do align your book-writing efforts with the focus of your freelance-writing business, or any of the "spoke" businesses that spin off from it, your book can be an important calling card that opens doors for new business opportunities.

Coaching. Business coaching is a service that helps executives and professionals achieve higher levels of performance. A personal trainer helps individuals develop and follow a fitness plan. Business coaches help professionals clarify business goals and create an action plan for achieving them. A coach provides support, validation, resources and accountability.

Many writers also become coaches. Assuming a writer has a writing niche, and subject matter expertise within that niche, then becoming a coach within that space is not that much of a leap. Some additional training and certification may be required to learn how to effectively coach clients, but the investment is worth it for many writers. While you may earn $100 per hour doing writing work, successful coaches typically earn two to four times that hourly rate.

Over the last few years, you may have noticed the surge in the number of people who are now offering coaching services—from life coaching to business coaching. Since there is no real barrier to entry in the form of a required degree or other certification, and coaching that is conducted virtually offers the prospect of earning a high hourly rate from the comfort of your home, it's attracting many people to the profession.

It's entirely possible for you to break into coaching as part of your transition to becoming a freelance writer, but don't expect it to be easy. While there is no required certification to call yourself a coach, you should invest in educating yourself on how to become an effective coach. Your education may involve a paid training program, or you may decide to self-educate using the many excellent books that teach various coaching techniques and methodologies.

Also, although not explicitly required, most effective coaches have at least some domain expertise related to the issues they're helping their coaching clients with. For example, coaches who purport to be capable of helping lawyers build legal practices should, in my opinion, have prior experience building a book of business as a lawyer (or at least as a professional in an adjacent field such as consulting). This may seem like common sense, but you would be surprised at the number of people who position themselves as coaches who have little to no experience in the domains and issues they're dealing with as a coach.

Consulting. After starting my writing career, I learned pretty quickly that the marketing and business development challenges my clients face run deeper than a lack of quality written content in the marketplace of ideas. Many have upstream challenges that are more fundamental, such as poor brand positioning or an ineffective website that doesn't convert traffic into leads. Others engage in random acts of marketing with no strategic marketing plan in place.

These and other client challenges presented obvious opportunities to expand my business beyond writing into various forms of marketing consulting. Not long after I started offering writing services, I began doing consulting work that helped significantly grow my business. The expansion of services allowed me to grow my team. Today, I have two partners, full-time graphic designers and account executives on staff, and freelance relationships with web developers and other writers who help tackle consulting projects for clients. We now offer a full suite of marketing services to clients. Writing is the "wheel" and we have a number of "spokes" in the form of additional marketing consulting services that generate a significant part of our revenue.

As you begin your writing business, you'll want to remain focused on expanding your writing client base. But you'll almost certainly start to recognize opportunities to add more value for your clients. Don't get distracted, and don't bite off more than you can chew, but don't be afraid to take on something that might feel like a stretch. Businesses grow by saying yes and figuring things out as they go.

A good place to start if you're looking to expand your services is to offer to help a client with a project that is similar to something you've done for yourself, such as setting up an email newsletter in MailChimp. In developing your brand, you may develop a relationship with a graphic designer you can bring into projects to help create a website or brochure for a client. In such instances, since you secured the work, you can pay the graphic designer and charge a marked-up rate for their services to the client.

Writing is the entry point to many marketing projects, and it's often not the only component that needs to get done. Be smart and strategic and think about ways you can move upstream to offer your clients more value—whether that's providing additional services yourself or connecting your client to other resources.

Moving beyond writing may not be your ambition, and there is obviously nothing wrong with staying in one lane. In fact, in many cases, that's the advisable route, because chasing too many opportunities often impedes progress. However, I believe it's important to paint the picture of what the future may hold for you, since many lawyers fail to pursue a new path due to limiting beliefs they harbor about what is possible in an alternative career.

If money is the sole driving force behind your decision making, then leaving the practice of law to become a writer is probably not the best option. But if you're not happy in your current circumstances, value the pursuit of passion and purpose more than money, and are excited by the prospect of a career with no predetermined path but lots of possibilities, then the writer's life may be for you.

CHAPTER 8

CONCLUSION

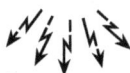

It's been close to a decade, but I still remember what it felt like to be a practicing lawyer. When someone learns that you're a lawyer, lame jokes aside, you gain instant respect. People ask your opinion. You're in a special cohort made up of smart professionals.

You and I know that much of the fascination and awe inspired by the legal profession is largely driven by unrealistic popular culture portrayals found in movies, television shows and novels. Nonetheless, there is a certain mystique associated with those who practice law.

That all went away the moment I left the law to become a writer. It would be dishonest for me to suggest that it wasn't hard to walk away. The sunk cost fallacy hit me hard. But as with most decisions in life, the worst-case scenario I envisioned (public shame, humiliation and abject poverty) didn't materialize—in fact, quite the opposite. Ten years later, I can't imagine things having gone any other way.

Becoming a writer is not easy. My main objective in writing this book is to provide an accurate picture of both the challenges and opportunities associated with the profession. Working for yourself is not easy. There are many times, to this day, when I fantasize about how much simpler my life would be if I didn't have to deal with things like making payroll and managing employees. But on balance, I wouldn't trade this life and this work for any other.

I know that some significant percentage of people who read this book will continue on their current path. And, despite how passionate I am about the benefits of pursuing a writing career, I'm okay with that. In fact, I'm extremely happy about it. Too often, people make rash decisions when they're feeling dissatisfied and jump straight from the frying pan into the fire. There is a tremendous amount of spammy, unreliable advice out there promising get-rich-quick schemes for work-from-home professionals. I'm not here to sell you snake oil.

If you're unhappy with your current circumstances as a practicing lawyer, perhaps what you need is a new job, not a new profession. If you're at a firm, you may be best served by trying another one, or working in a corporate legal department. Maybe contract legal work is a better fit than a full-time job with a single employer. In short, the advice in this book is not for everyone.

But it is for someone. Maybe for you?

You may be among the countless number of lawyers who are looking for something new. You may be in a position, such as being a parent of young children, that simply does not allow you to keep up with the pace of the practice of law—at least in this season of your life. You may be someone who is looking to take a step back to evaluate what comes next in your career, but you want to stay intellectually stimulated, earn money, and continue to put your hard-earned skills to productive use. You may have no qualms whatsoever and be dead certain that the writer's life is right for you.

For me, the most valuable part of switching careers was that I finally felt, for the first time in my professional life, that my work was aligned with my purpose. I was stimulated by my work and my clients valued it. That was often missing when I practiced law.

That being said, my experience may not be yours. I know many lawyers who are energized, fulfilled and happy in their legal careers. Hooray for that! We need enthusiastic lawyers. But it's equally important to identify paths forward for the rest of us.

In 1916, Robert Frost published one of the most renowned poems of the 20th Century, "The Road Not Taken," which begins: "Two roads diverged in a yellow wood..." The metaphor of the "fork in the road," upon which Frost's seminal work is based, is so enduring because it is so universal. Every day, each one of us is confronted with choices, big and small, that determine the direction of our lives and careers.

In most cases, particularly when it comes to the "big" choices in life, each path is distinctly marked. There is the easy, default path, and the hard, purposeful path. Too often, people look back on their lives and realize that many of the actions they took (or didn't), choices they made (or didn't), and priorities they set (or didn't) happened by default; guided by the expectations of society and others, and not by their own inner compass. They traveled the safe, smooth path, not the uneven, winding one, and ultimately reached a destination, but one they regret in the end.

We all grapple with regret stemming from the choices we make (or don't) in our lives. What's important to realize, however, is that at any point in life's journey, if you can summon the courage, you can stop, assess and change direction. The key to making positive change, to living a life free of regret and full of passion, is to open yourself up to what truly matters—to you, not others—and to embrace the risks involved in pursuing it. After all, isn't the risk of not living a life true to yourself an even greater risk?

According to Mark Twain: "The two most important days in your life are the day you are born and the day you find out why."

What is your *Why*? What path holds the most promise for you? Only you can answer these questions. There is no certainty of outcome. But recognize that not making a choice is, itself, a choice. Will you choose to become a writer?

CONCLUSION

OUTLAW WRITER ACADEMY

——

You've read the book—now take action to start and grow your freelance-writing business as a member of the OutLaw Writer Academy. The OutLaw Writer Academy is a virtual workshop for aspiring freelance writers in which Jay Harrington guides members through the process of getting their businesses off the ground, gaining traction with clients, and earning meaningful income from their writing.

From positioning to pricing strategies, you'll get expert guidance and helpful resources that take the guesswork out of becoming a successful freelance writer. Best of all, you'll be part of an engaged community of other OutLaw writers who provide each other support, resources, and inspiration. Learn more about OutLaw Writer Academy at **www.outlawwriter.com**.

ABOUT THE AUTHOR

I am an attorney, author, executive coach and trainer, and marketing consultant. This is my fourth book. My first book, *One of a Kind: A Proven Path to a Profitable Law Practice*, was published by Attorney at Work in 2016. *The Essential Associate: Step Up, Stand Out, and Rise to the Top as a Young Lawyer* was published in 2018. *The Productivity Pivot: Build a Profitable Legal Practice by Selling Yourself One Hour Every Day* was released in 2020. In addition to my writing and consulting, I frequently speak and conduct training workshops at law firm retreats, bar association gatherings, and other legal industry events.

I live in the beautiful small town of Traverse City, Michigan, with my wife and three young daughters. Outside of work and spending time with family and friends, I enjoy hiking, biking, paddle boarding, golfing and skiing.

Previously I was a commercial litigator and corporate

bankruptcy attorney at Skadden, Arps, Slate, Meagher & Flom in Chicago, and Foley & Lardner in Detroit. I also co-founded a boutique corporate bankruptcy firm in metro Detroit in 2009.

In 2006, I co-founded Harrington Communications, one of the nation's leading legal marketing and public relations agencies. I am part of a team of creative professionals serving the marketing and communications needs of a national client base of leading law firms. I also provide business development coaching and training to lawyers.

I earned my law degree from the University of Michigan Law School in 2001, and played baseball (and, yes, studied) at Bowling Green State University. I had the good fortune of competing in the College World Series regional tournament in 1998 (although we were knocked out of the tournament by the number-one ranked University of Miami Hurricanes).

You can read more of my writing on my blog at **www.hcommunications.biz**. In addition, I encourage you to check out my weekly podcast, The Thought Leadership Podcast, which you can find at **www.thethoughtleadershipproject.com**.

ACKNOWLEDGMENTS

Writing a book requires a team effort. I am grateful to the people who supported me throughout the process.

Thank you to my wife, Heather, and our three daughters. As always, I'm deeply appreciative of the work Tom Nixon puts in to read and improve my book drafts.

I could not have done this without you!

NOTES

Introduction

https://www.upwork.com/press/2017/10/17/freelanc-ing-in-america-2017/

Chapter 1

https://www.americanbar.org/groups/lawyer_assistance/research/colap_hazelden_lawyer_study/

https://www.psychologytoday.com/us/blog/bounc-ing-back/201106/the-no-1-contributor-happiness

https://www.jgrisham.com/bio/

https://www.nytimes.com/2002/09/28/opinion/think-you-have-a-book-in-you-think-again.html

Chapter 2

https://psycnet.apa.org/buy/1995-05382-001

https://www.alphavoice.io/video/the-tim-ferris-show/442-tribe-of-mentors-naval-ravikant-susan-cain-and-yuval-no-ah-harari

Chapter 3

https://www.dominican.edu/dominicannews/study-high-lights-strategies-for-achieving-goals

www.ingramcontent.com/pod-product-compliance
Lightning Source LLC
Chambersburg PA
CBHW050510210326
41521CB00011B/2395